Classical Guitar of Fernando Sor

CONTENTS

Biographical Notes on Arranger-Joseph Harris 2

Historical Notes & Performance Suggestions 3

Variations on a Theme from Mozart's "The Magic Flute," Op. 9 12

Waltz in C Major, Op. 18, No. 6 23

Minuet in D Major, Op. 11, No. 5 26

Minuet in E Major, Op. 11, No. 10 28

Divertimento in C Major, Op. 13, No. 3 31

Les Folies d'Espangne, Op. 15(a) 34

Six Airs from Mozart's "The Magic Flute," Op. 19 40

Fantasia in E Minor, Op. 21 ("Les Adieux") 54

Minuet in C Major, from Grand Sonata, Op. 22 62

Petite Piece in A Major, Op. 45, No. 3 66

Study in D Major, Op. 29, No. 21 71

Petite Piece in A Major, Op. 45, No. 5 72

Minuet in G Major (c. 1810) 78

Bagatelle in D Minor, Op. 43, No. 5 80

Study in E Minor, Op. 6, No. 11 83

Lecon in D Major, Op. 31, No. 10 90

Lecon in E Major, Op. 31, No. 23 92

Petite Piece in E Major, Op. 32, No. 1 94

Study in B Minor, Op. 35, No. 22 96

Minuet in G Major, Op. 2, No. 1 99

Petite Piece in A Major, Op. 44, No. 21 100

Minuet in A Major, Op. 11, No. 6 102

ISBN 978-0-634-03082-2

EXCLUSIVELY DISTRIBUTED BY
HAL•LEONARD®
CORPORATION
7777 W. BLUEMOUND RD. P.O. BOX 13819 MILWAUKEE, WI 53213

Visit Hal Leonard Online at
www.halleonard.com

ABOUT THE ARRANGER

Joseph Harris received his bachelor's and master's degrees in guitar performance at Northern Arizona University as a student of Tom Sheeley. Joseph has done further graduate study in music theory at the University of Iowa. In addition to his work with the classical guitar, his musical pursuits include jazz guitar, music aesthetics and the music of French composer Olivier Messiaen (1908-1992). In his spare time Joseph enjoys camping, canoeing, spelunking and rock climbing.

Historical Notes & Performance Suggestions

Fernando Sor and "The Golden Age of the Guitar"

Music historians often refer to the first half of the nineteenth century as "the golden age of the guitar." During this time the guitar enjoyed an unprecedented popularity. Audiences assembled in masses to see great guitarists in concert. Professionals and enthusiasts alike engaged in spirited debates over the nature of the guitar and its players. This period saw the circulation of the first magazine devoted to the guitar, the *Guilianiad* (which despite being named after the well-known virtuoso Mauro Giuliani promoted the talents of many guitarists). Most significantly, the guitar found its way into the homes of the middle class. Due to a flourishing market for guitar music aimed toward amateur players, many of them women, the sound of the guitar was heard everywhere including in the streets, in the salon as well as on the concert stage.

Among the most-praised musicians of the golden age of the guitar was Fernando Sor. With the age's excitement for the guitar in full bloom, Sor burst onto the scene when his compositional and performance skills were fully developed. Everywhere he went he was received with unabashed enthusiasm and lauded with the highest honors. Like all guitarists of his time, Sor played upon a guitar that was much smaller and weaker in tone than today's instruments. However, armed with this crude, diminutive guitar and fueled with an immense musical passion, Sor created music that towered above his contemporaries and today stands as an enduring monument to his devotion, dedication and love for the instrument.

Sor's Early Musical Development

When Sor first began his musical lessons under his father in Barcelona, Spain, the guitar was not popularly recognized as a concert instrument. Sor's family held more conservative expectations for their son, hoping that he would pursue a career in the Spanish military. Sor's earliest formal schooling was at the monastery at Montserrat. The monks actually provided Sor with a fair amount of musical training, even though they were unable to provide any lessons on the guitar. At the monastery's famous choir school Sor learned about singing and the fundamentals of musicianship. Despite the curriculum, Sor maintained his passion for the guitar while at the monastery, so that when he left he continued to pursue the development of his talents upon the instrument.

Sor did end up pursuing a military career, and eventually received a military commission, all the while never abandoning his musical aspirations. While stationed in Madrid, Sor enjoyed the patronage of the Duchess of Alba, who supported many musicians and artists including painter Francisco Goya. The Duchess brought Sor under her wing and encouraged him to develop his musical talents. Quite fortunately for Sor, the Duchess was rather lenient compared to other patrons of the arts; instead of requiring him to compose exclusively for her court, she lavished him with a room in her house, books and other supplies, and let him study and compose whatever he desired.

Sor as Spanish Exile

In 1813, Sor left his native Spain, due to a rather uncomfortable political situation. He and many others (including Goya) had allied themselves with the French cause during a period of French occupation. When the Spanish overthrew the puppet king, Joseph Bonaparte (Napoleans's brother), *afrancesados* such as Sor found themselves in a difficult position and were forced to leave Spain. Sor relocated to Paris, which in the nineteenth century was the European hub of artistic and intellectual activity and home to many towering figures including Hector Berlioz, Victor Hugo, Honoré de Balzac and Eugène Delacroix.

Although opera virtually dominated the Parisian musical climate in the first half of the nineteenth century, the guitar enjoyed an immense popularity. In fact, Paris showed more of an interest in the guitar than any other European city. Parisians were extremely receptive to Sor's arrival, keeping him in great demand as a composer and a performer. Later in life, Sor was also in great demand in Paris as a teacher. Paris was Sor's home for a large part of his life and was the city where he composed the majority of his guitar works.

After his initial move to Paris, Sor traveled extensively throughout Europe. He visited Germany, Russia and England with major stops in Berlin, Warsaw, Moscow, St. Petersburg and London. Sor's music met with great success wherever he traveled. He was particularly well-received in London—Sor was the first and only guitarist to have the honor to perform with the London Philharmonic during its first one hundred years. In 1826, while in St. Petersburg, he was called upon to compose a march for the funeral of Tsar Alexander. In the late 1820s, he ceased touring and spent the rest of his life in Paris. Due to political tensions, Sor was never able to return home to his native Spain.

Sor's Compositions

Although Sor composed music for a variety of mediums, his most enduring works are those for the guitar. His hundreds of guitar compositions generally fall into three categories: works intended to satisfy the public's demand for technically undemanding yet pleasing music suitable for the salon or home, works designed for one's technical improvement on the instrument (études, leçons and the like) and larger works designed for Sor's own performances.

An event which cemented Sor's position as one of the most respected guitarists of the day was the publication of his *Methode pour la guitare* ("Method for the Guitar") in 1830. The book is an exposition of Sor's beliefs on proper guitar technique and musicianship. The underlying tone of Sor's presentation is one of the utmost thoughtfulness, assiduousness and sensibility. In his book, Sor constantly reminds the reader that the precepts he advocates are the results of critical thinking. At the very beginning of his book, Sor boldly asserts an anti-dogmatic stance by stating that the contents of his book are based on his own reflections and experience and do not blindly follow anyone else's maxims. The book contains relatively little music—indeed, it was more likely intended to illustrate Sor's approach to the instrument than to serve as a primer. On the whole, the book serves as an illuminating insight into Sor's musical aesthetics and into his criticisms of contemporary guitar playing.

In addition to guitar works, Sor was a composer of seguidillas (Spanish songs modeled on the dance of the same name), Spanish patriotic songs, piano pieces, ballets, operas and other large orchestral works. Outside of his guitar music, Sor enjoyed the most success with his operas and ballets; his ballet *Cendrillon* was performed over one hundred times during the 1820s. Sor's last large orchestral work was a Mass in memory of his daughter, who suffered an untimely passing during the summer of 1837. Perhaps Sor's most unusual musical endeavor was the composition of a few pieces for an unpopular instrument called the harpolyre, an invention of English musician J.F. Salomon. The harpolyre was basically a triple-neck acoustic guitar, with a total of 21 strings of various materials. Understandably, the sensation of this musical oddity died in 1831 along with its inventor.

The Legacy of Fernando Sor

Sor was not the only nineteenth-century composer with a passion for the guitar. Carl Maria von Weber, Franz Schubert and Hector Berlioz all played the guitar. Unfortunately, these great composers left extremely little, if any, music for the instrument. (Many of Schubert's early songs were initially conceived with guitar accompaniment; however, Schubert later reworked the accompaniments for piano.

In his *Grand traité d'instrumentation et d'orchestration modernes* ("Great treatise on instrumentation and modern orchestration"), Berlioz goes so far as to include the guitar in his concept of the ideal orchestra. Nevertheless, the guitar never seemed to make its way into Berlioz's orchestral works.)

In addition to Sor, those who left the most indelible mark on the instrument during the golden age of the guitar were other guitarist-composers: Dioniso Aguado (a close friend of Sor), Ferdinando Carulli, Matteo Carcassi and Mauro Giuliani. Sor stands out among his contemporaries due to the fact that he was the only guitarist-composer whose works consistently remained in favor with audiences and performers.

One of the most incredible aspects of Sor's guitar compositions is the fact that they are simultaneously well-crafted musically yet perfectly suited to the instrument. The exquisite craftsmanship of his music most certainly is due in a large part to his formidable training by the monks in Montserrat. Divorced from the instrument, Sor's harmonic progressions, melodic lines, textures and voice-leading make perfect musical sense. Even so, the music sings on the guitar with a brilliance and a vitality unattainable with any other instrument.

Minuet in G Major, Op. 2, No. 1

A typical minuet has a clear structure with regular four-bar phrases, and this early Minuet of Sor is no exception. When playing this piece, think of each four-bar phrase as a distinct musical idea. Give each phrase its own shape and musical direction. The overall form of the piece is quite refined—at sixteen bars in length, the piece contains only four phrases.

Notwithstanding its brevity, this simple Minuet allows for quite a bit of expressive interpretation. Aim for a wide dynamic spectrum. Use a rich, dark tone, and dig the fingers into the strings as much as possible. Keep the character elegant and stately, and keep the tempo lively.

Study in E Minor, Op. 6, No. 11

Many of Sor's studies exercise a particular aspect of guitar technique. The Study in E Minor, Op. 6, No. 11 is meant to improve the guitarist's skill at playing arpeggios.

Although the musical surface of the Study is quite active, the melody is drawn out in long notes. Emphasize the notes of the melody (which are indicated with upstems) with rest strokes. The melody in the Study should sing with the expressive and lilting qualities of the human voice.

Be sure to follow the indicated right hand fingerings; the thumb of the right hand is used sparingly throughout. When the piece switches mode to the parallel major (mm. 58 to the end), use a contrasting tone color.

Variations on a Theme form Mozart's The Magic Flute, Op. 9

This incendiary piece is Sor's best-known and most-performed work. The actual tune that the variations are based on is from the charming duet "Das klinget so herrlich," taken from the finale to the first act of Mozart's opera *The Magic Flute*. Be sure to compare the Variations, Op. 9 with Sor's Six Airs form Mozart's *The Magic Flute*, Op. 19 (also in this book). The fourth air is based on the same tune as the Variations; however, the Airs are light salon pieces, while the Variations serve as a vehicle for technical display.

This piece is a good example of nineteenth-century bravura, a term used to describe music of an extroverted character that is meant to dazzle the listener with seemingly impossible feats of technique, when in actual fact is not that difficult to play. Be sure to have fun with this piece. Feel free to push the tempo for effect, especially in the final variation.

Sor's too-often ignored introduction is included in this book. The introduction may seem to stand in stark contrast to the rest of the work, but it is actually essential because it presents many significant musical ideas that appear later in the variations. The introduction prepares the Variations' tonality of E. The minor mode and thick chord voicings of the variations return in the second variation. Most notably, the introduction presents repeated notes on the open second string, a motive that appears throughout the variations. The fact that the introduction's somber character contrasts with the bright and lively character of the variations can actually work to the performer's advantage. Feel free to play this fantasia-like introduction with plenty of rubato. Linger slightly on the harmonics in mm. 16–19, since these notes stop ringing as soon as the next note is struck. Throughout the variations, keep the pull-offs clean.

Minuet in D Major, Op. 11, No. 5

Unlike the Minuet from the Grand Sonata, Op. 22 (also in this book), the Minuet Op. 11, No. 5 does not exist within the scope of a larger work. This freestanding piece was published as part of a small set of minuets.

The most technically challenging aspect of the Minuet is the alternating bass pattern in the right hand thumb. Particularly tricky examples are in mm. 9–12 and 17–20. Such patterns are commonly found in modern bluegrass music (totally unknown to Sor, of course). However, Sor challenges the player by placing the low notes (usually found on the downbeats) on the upbeats. Play the downstemmed eighth notes with the thumb; play all the other notes with the fingers. The coordination required for these passages is easily attainable at a reduced tempo, so start slowly and push the tempo as the fingerings become more comfortable.

Minuet in A Major, Op. 11, No. 6

This early work of Sor seems to reveal a glimpse of Sor's Spanish heritage. A passionate and fiery Iberian temperament is suggested in the juxtaposition of sudden energetic outbursts, rapidly flung arpeggios and ultra-sweet melodic turns.

The Minuet contains a couple of passages that would feel quite natural on Sor's tiny guitar, but which require a bit of a left-hand stretch when played on a modern guitar. For the stretch in mm. 5–6, keep the left hand as relaxed as possible. To sweeten this passage, as per its marking of *dolce*, add a bit of vibrato.

Overall, keep the tempo and character energetic, but restrained. Even through there are a lot of passages with fast notes, don't let the tempo get out of hand. Play the arpeggios in mm. 13–15 smoothly and evenly, with a slight crescendo towards the end. Sor's magnificent gift for melody is evident in this short Minuet. Take special care to make the melody sing as much as possible, especially when it is unaccompanied. Keep all of the grace notes and ornaments light and quick.

Minuet in E Major, Op. 11, No. 10

This piece demonstrates Sor's ability to take what would ordinarily be a simple genre piece and transform it into a tour-de-force of technique and musical drama. From the opening march-like rhythms to the rapid, wide-voiced arpeggios at the close, the piece contains a variety of motives and textures, constantly alternating between brilliant displays of technique and serene moments of repose.

This piece sounds well with a true rubato—don't play with a disregard to tempo, but slow down in certain places and speed up in others. For example, in m. 15, linger slightly on the dotted note on the downbeat, then slightly accelerate the accompanimental notes in the later part of the measure. The bravura pull-offs in mm. 27 and 29 are similar to those found in other works of Sor, including his Variations on a Theme from Mozart's *The Magic Flute*, Op. 9 (also in this book). Keep these pull-offs clean and quick.

Divertimento in C Major, Op. 13, No. 3

This charming piece most certainly was intended to satiate the musical appetites of the amateur guitarists that inhabited nineteenth-century Parisian salons. The word "divertimento" literally means "amusement," suggesting that both guitarist and listener would find the piece entertaining.

This particular Divertimento is in the form of a minuet, a stately dance in triple meter and moderate tempo. Placing a slight accent on the downbeat will contribute to a dance-like feeling. Keep the character elegant and graceful, and make the melody sing.

Measures 33 to the end are a reprise of the opening sixteen measures, but with embellishments in the form of diminutions. Make sure the tempo of each section is approximately the same—don't slow down for the fast notes. The middle section (mm. 17–32), in the parallel minor, contrasts the outer sections. Here, it would be appropriate to slow down the tempo a bit and play with a darker tone color and a hint of rubato.

Les Folies d'Espagne, Op. 15(a)

The song "Folies d'Espagne" had been used as the basis for composition by countless composers before Sor, including many fellow Spanish guitarists. Traditionally, the composer uses the song as the basis of a repeated harmonic ground, upon which are composed variations. Each variation exhibits different motives, textures and rhythms while remaining true to the harmonic ground.

This piece is very much in the mood of a variation form of a sixteenth-century Spanish vihuelist. The variations are continuous (there are no indicated pauses between variations), the tempo is consistent, and the stratified voices within the musical texture contain a relatively equal amount of melodic activity. Be sure to bring out any moving voices while retaining a sense of polyphony. As this piece contains many moving chords, in the manner of parallel thirds and the like, be sure to hold each chord for as long as possible and avoid a staccato-like sound.

Waltz in C Major, Op. 18, No. 6

This formally simple piece must have found its way into many Parisian salons in the nineteenth century. This Waltz echoes strains of Vienna, which in the nineteenth century was a major center of interest in the guitar, second only to Paris.

In mm. 17–18, it would be appropriate to bring out the dissonances on the downbeat. Accent these notes slightly and give each a slight tenuto. Keep the meter of this Waltz brisk, graceful and dance-like. Keeping with nineteenth-century music performance practice, be sure to begin the trills (mm. 33–34 and 52–53) with the lower note.

Six Airs from Mozart's *The Magic Flute*, Op. 19

Opera was the staple of the Parisian musical diet in the first half of the nineteenth century. In fact, opera was the dominating force of nearly all aspects of Parisian musical culture. Of course, in the nineteenth century, practically the only way to bring concert music, including operatic music, into one's own home was through arrangements for household instruments such as the guitar. In Six Airs from Mozart's *The Magic Flute*, Sor prepares a few highlights from the opera. Here, a consumer could experience the grandeur of large-scale work by a great master, but reduced to manageable proportions. Although such arrangements were often conceived primarily as money-makers for publishing houses, the Airs are quite deserving of the concert stage.

For the solemn tone of the first and sixth movements, keep the tempo even and play the chords with a full, rich tone. In the third movement, keep the ornaments quick and light.

The third and fourth movements contain numerous harmonics. Since harmonics tend to sound with a much more subdued tone (especially those produced above the third and fourth frets), strike these notes with more force; likewise, bring down the volume of the fretted notes in these passages so that the dynamic level remains consistent.

Be sure to compare the fourth movement, "O dolce harmonia," to Sor's Variations on a Theme from Mozart's *The Magic Flute* (also in this book). Both are based on exactly the same music, but the Variations are much more technically brilliant while the Airs remain more true to the music of Mozart's opera.

Fantasia in E Minor, Op. 21 ("Les Adieux")

Although François Joseph Fetis's description of Fernando Sor as "the Beethoven of the guitar" is neither accurate nor appropriate, there is one indisputable similarity between the two composers: they both composed a substantial work with the title "Les Adieux." Beethoven completed his Sonata for Piano No. 26 in E-flat, Op. 81a ("Les Adieux") in 1810; Sor's Fantasia in E Minor, Op. 21 ("Les Adieux") was first published a few years later, in 1825. While Sor's music never exhibits a Romantic sensibility to the same degree as Beethoven's music does, Sor's Fantasia does contain quite a bit of introspection, pathos and musical drama. In fact, the only thing that seems to be denying the Fantasia a Beethoven-like status is its relatively small scope. No sooner is the mood of the first half of the piece established when it quickly dwindles away and gives way to the second half. (This isn't to suggest that Sor was incapable of producing large-scale works. One only need look to his two Guitar Sonatas, Opp. 22 and 25, to find full-blown multi-movemented works.)

Be sure to provide the Fantasia with a wide range of contrasts, especially in terms of dynamics and tone colors. Keep the tempo of the second half, "Un poco mosso," rather fast. The Fantasia's textures are quite active throughout; nevertheless, be sure to emphasize the melodic lines at all times.

Minuet, from *Grand Sonata in C Major*, Op. 22

Although sonatas for guitar do not figure greatly in Sor's output, the two that he did produce are among the boldest in scope compared to those of his contemporaries. The Grand Sonata, Op. 22 is in four movements: an opening Allegro, a slow Adagio, a dancelike Minuet, and a Rondo for the finale. The inclusion of the entire Sonata would be beyond the compass of this book; however, the Minuet is included in order to provide a taste of the more academic side of Sor. The formal outlines of the Minuet are extremely clear: phrases are each exactly four measures in length, and except for a very brief nod to the relative minor in mm. 9–11, the tonality never strays far from C major.

When performing the Minuet, keep the character lively and dancelike yet elegant and gracious. Many of the slurs are quite friendly to the guitar—it is easy to speed up in these passages, so make sure to exercise restraint and execute the slurred notes with rhythmic precision.

Study in D Major, Op. 29, No. 21

Along with his *Methode*, Sor's studies for the guitar were among the most popular of his guitar works during the nineteenth century, even well after his death. Sor's studies are indeed "concert études," meaning they are as much at home on the concert stage as in the salon.

This curious Study is to be played entirely in natural harmonics. Sor was fascinated by harmonics on the guitar. In fact, he devoted a chapter of his *Methode* to the study of harmonics, and devised intricate charts that demonstrated all the harmonics possible on the guitar.

Pay particular attention to the tablature staff when studying this piece. While it is not uncommon to find twelfth-fret, seventh-fret and fifth-fret harmonics in guitar music, many of the harmonics in this study are found at the third, fourth and ninth frets. Because of their relative location in the overtone series, these particular harmonics sound quite weak, so be sure to play them with great force. Play these weak notes with rest strokes whenever possible. Also, striking the string with the tip of the fingernail will give these notes a brighter and more penetrating tone.

Sometimes, the melody note is played on a lower string than the rest of the chord. (An example is the first chord of m. 2, where the melody note A is played on the fourth string, while the F-sharp, sounding a minor third lower, is played on the second string.) In such instances, you will have to strike each string with a different degree of force; be sure to play the melody note with enough force so that it is not drowned out by the accompanimental note.

Leçon in D Major, Op. 31, No. 10

The guitar pieces that Sor wrote with didactic intentions exhibit different generic titles. A subtle difference exists between what Sor calls a "leçon" and what he calls an "étude." The leçon (lesson) is usually intended for a beginning student or amateur guitarist, and tends to offer practice for the guitarist in terms of general musicianship and note reading. The étude (study), on the other hand, requires more virtuosity and usually isolates a specific technique. While the leçon would be most at home in a private performance in the salon, the proper venue for the étude is the concert stage.

Even though this Leçon is quite simple technically, it carries a great amount of expressive potential. Make sure the melody sounds sweet and lyrical. Perform with plenty of vibrato everywhere. Sor's tempo designation *Cantabile* indicates that the melody should convey the lyrical qualities of a vocal line.

Make sure that the thirds and sixths in mm. 21–22 sound very legato. In m. 23, hold the E on the downbeat through beat two—don't lift the first finger until the beginning of beat three. In mm. 9–12, don't let the moving inner voices overpower the melody in the soprano.

Leçon in E Major, Op. 31, No. 23

Like the Leçon, Op. 31, No. 10, this technically undemanding piece requires a great deal of attention in order to sound musically convincing. The tempo marking *Mouvement de prière religieuse* (Tempo of a religious prayer) suggests a slow and solemn tempo. Hold on to the notes of each chord for as long as possible. Play with a warm, dark tone color, and maintain a strong and forceful sound.

Petite Pièce in E Major, Op. 32, No. 1

Keep the character of this Petite Pièce elegant and graceful, and maintain a steady, even tempo. The Petite Pièce contains many groupettes (triplet in m. 6, quintuplet in mm. 14 and 26, and sextuplets in mm. 10, 30 and 31). Don't worry too much about executing the groupettes with rhythmic precision— treat them more as ornamental upbeats to the next measure. In mm. 17–20, a contrasting tone color would be appropriate.

Study in B Minor, Op. 35, No. 22

Like the Study in E Minor, Op. 6, No. 11, this Study has a very straightforward intent: to improve the guitarist's ability to play arpeggios. The right hand fingering remains straightforward throughout, while the left hand rarely moves above second position.

Emphasize the melody notes (on beats one and three, for the most part) with rest strokes. This simple Study actually holds the potential for a fair amount of musical drama. When performing the Study, at all times be aware of melodic direction. In this piece, exceptionally expressive moments are right before cadences, such as in mm. 29–32 and 41–44. Be sure to play these passages with plenty of expression—these are the moments that the audience will remember the most.

Bagatelle in D Minor, Op. 43, No. 5

Many of Sor's character pieces seem to have been directed towards public consumption. The title of the Op. 45 set, "Mes Ennuis" ("My Boredoms"), and the title "Bagatelle" (literally, a "trifle") perfectly suggest the mood of a nineteenth-century middle-class Parisian debutante. The Bagatelle would be sure to offer a pleasant musical diversion to anyone's day.

The fingerings are ever-so-slightly unconventional, but still quite manageable. In the first half of the Bagatelle (mm. 1–16), be sure to play the chords with a full tone, digging the flesh of the fingertip into the string as far as possible. In the second half (m. 17 to the end), bring out the melody hidden in the arpeggiations (indicated with upstems). A good way to do this is to play the melody notes with rest strokes.

Petite Pièce in A Major, Op. 44, No. 21

In his *Methode pour la guitare* , Sor often reminds the reader of the attention required to make a melody executed on the guitar sound as singing as possible. Indeed, the guitar as an instrument is totally incapable of producing a true legato sound. Once a tone is sounded on the guitar, it immediately begins to decay and to die away. Therefore, the guitarist must make use of whatever tricks are available in order to give the illusion of a seamless, supple melody. As with the minuets in this book, each phrase of the Petite Pièce is exactly four bars in length. Each phrase must be executed with a sense of forward motion in order to properly convey the broad musical structure. Imagine each phrase as a long arch, with the short-term goal being the cadence at the end of the phrase.

The texture of this piece is quite consistent throughout—one could easily imagine it being played by a string trio. When performing this Petite Pièce, be thinking constantly of the true legato capabilities of bowed string instruments. Hold on to each note for as long as possible, especially in passages containing thirds (as in mm. 9–15). Strive for zero separation between successive notes. The most attractive feature of the Petite Pièce is its graceful melody. Play the melody with plenty of expression, while keeping it within the shape of each phrase. Keep the atmosphere of the Pièce delicate, but warm, and use much vibrato throughout.

Petite Pièce in A Major, Op. 45, No. 3

This Petite Pièce ("Small Piece") belies its name. Because of its many repeats, this Pièce actually takes quite a long time to perform. Perhaps the title is meant to refer to the actual amount of "new" material the guitarist encounters.

The Pièce contains many sumptuously voiced harmonies (especially in the first few measures), so be sure to play with a full, warm tone and with lots of vibrato. In the middle section, many of the notes are played on the open first and second strings. Be especially careful to play these notes with plenty of warmth, to compensate for the characteristically dead sound of the open string.

Petite Pièce in A Major, Op. 45, No. 5

Sor's Op. 45, No. 5 is another "Small Piece" that betrays its name. However, the repetitions in this Pièce are often varied, creating unexpected yet pleasant surprises for both the player and the listener. The most common technique of variation in this Pièce is through a method of embellishment called "diminution," wherein the composer modifies the pre-existing melody by inserting notes of smaller (diminished) durations. A striking example is m. 75 (a recomposition of m. 19). Here Sor replaces the eighth notes of the melody with an entire measure of thirty-second notes. (Notice, though, that Sor compensates for this increased melodic activity by reducing the number of notes in the accompaniment.)

In order to give the Pièce more shape, perform the middle section (mm. 33–64) with a contrasting character. This section, in the parallel minor, would sound appropriate with a warm, dark tone color.

Minuet in G Major (c. 1810)

This delightful Minuet is one of the few guitar works of Sor that was never assigned an opus number. The Minuet actually exists in more than one version. The version in this book is taken from a set of four minuets of Sor published in the short-lived Parisian periodical *Journal de musique etrangère pour la guitar ou lyre* ("Journal of Foreign Music for the Guitar or "Lyre"). (Remember that in 1810 Sor, a Spaniard, was still considered a "foreigner" to the French.) These minuets represent the very first printed editions of the guitar music of Sor. In fact, Sor did not begin to formally publish his guitar compositions until after he had arrived in Paris in 1813.

The Minuet suggests a lively tempo, so some of the passages (especially the passages in parallel thirds, as in the first measure) will require extra practice in order to sound smooth and legato. Isolate these passages and practice them extremely slowly, out of tempo, with the left-hand thumb off the neck, with liberal amounts of vibrato and above all with minimal tension in the body. After a few days the difficult passages will seem to play themselves.

Although this piece lends itself very well to dynamic extremes, overall maintain a strong dynamic level, making sure the difficult passages sound bold yet fluid.

Variations on a Theme from
Mozart's *The Magic Flute*
Op. 9

Edited and fingered by
Joseph Harris

Fernando Sor
(1778–1839)

Introduction

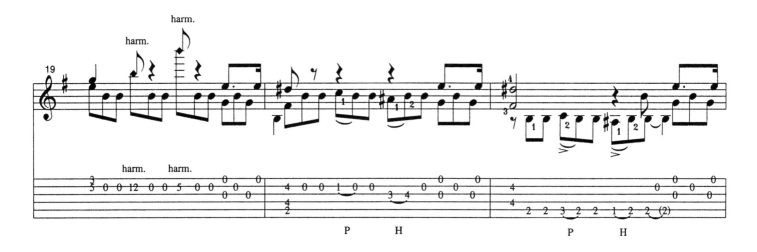

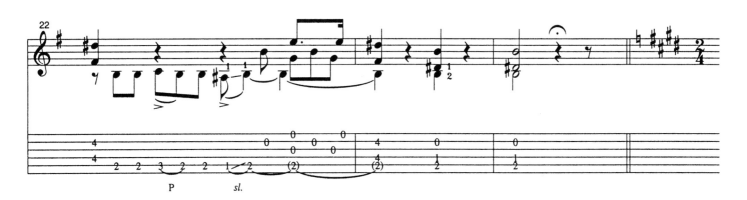

Theme

Andante moderato

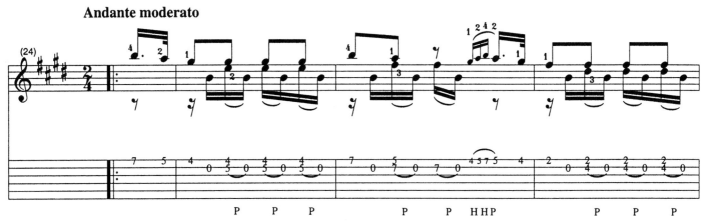

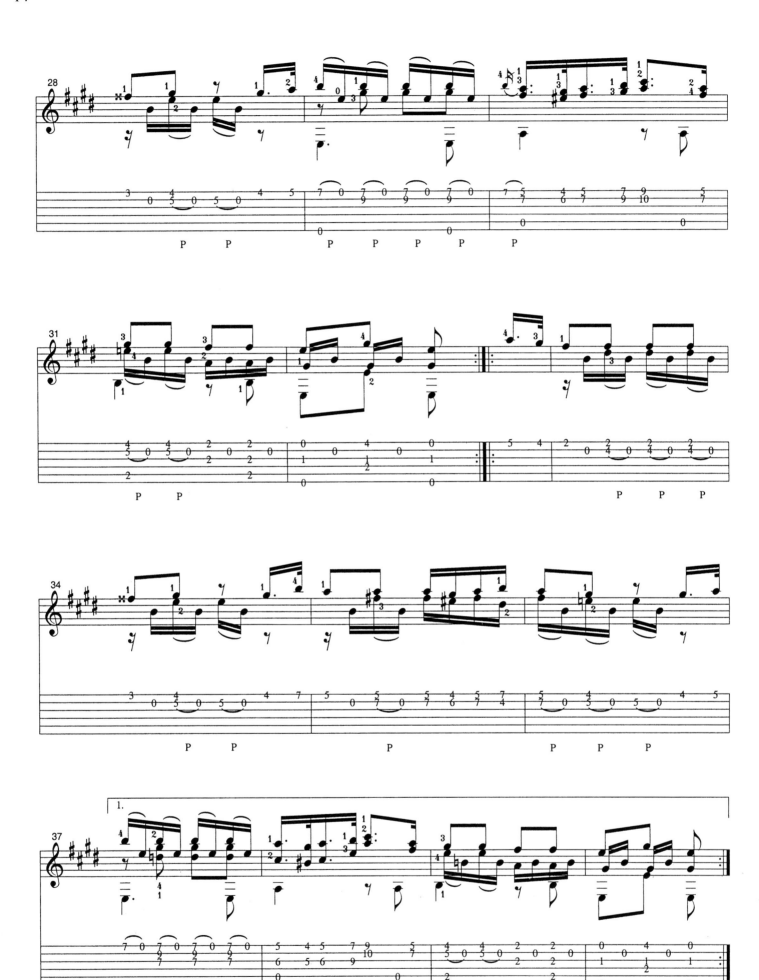

First variation

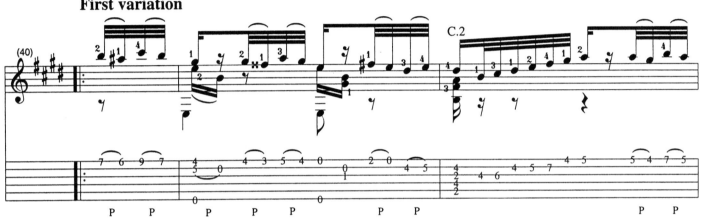

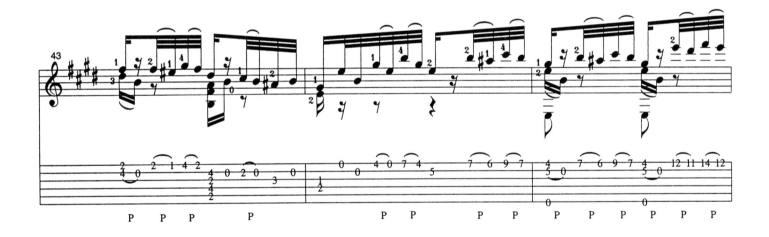

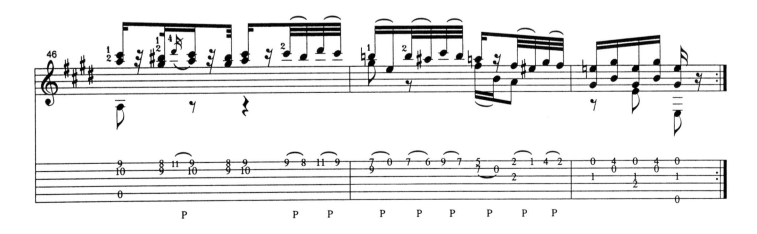

Second variation

PPH

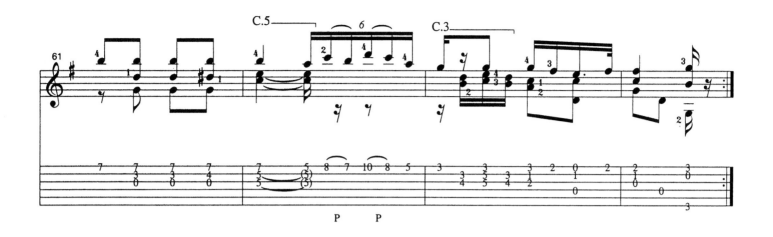

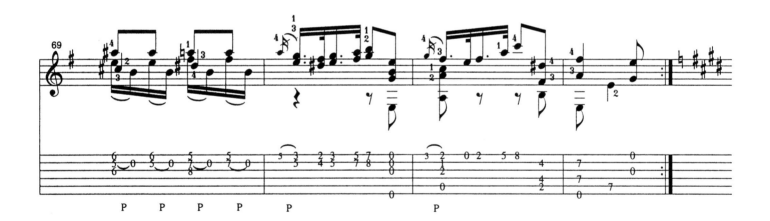

Third variation

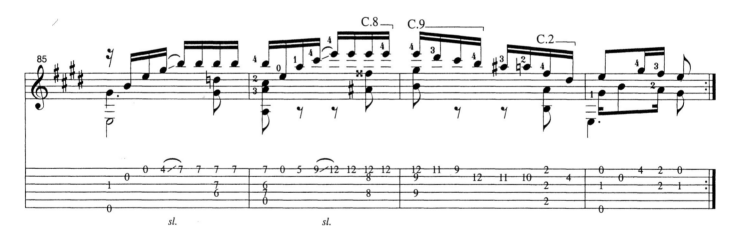

Fourth variation

Più mosso

Fifth variation

Più mosso

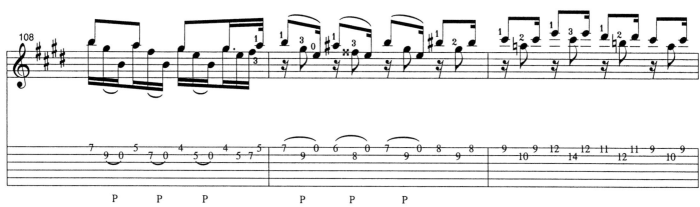

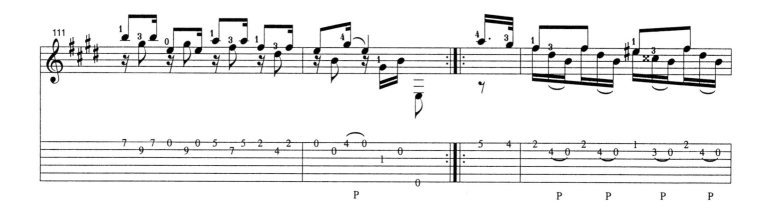

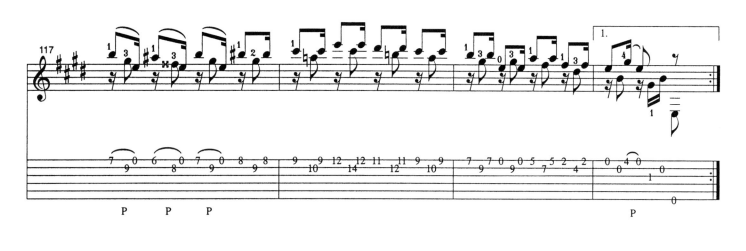

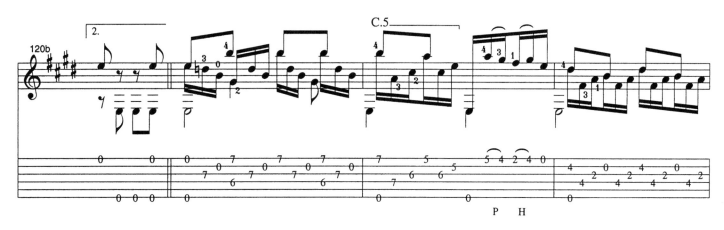

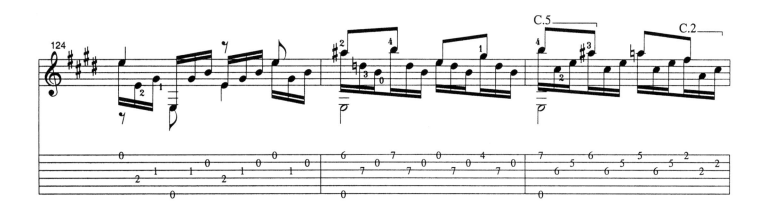

Waltz in C Major
Op. 18, No. 6

Edited and fingered by
Joseph Harris

Fernando Sor
(1778–1839)

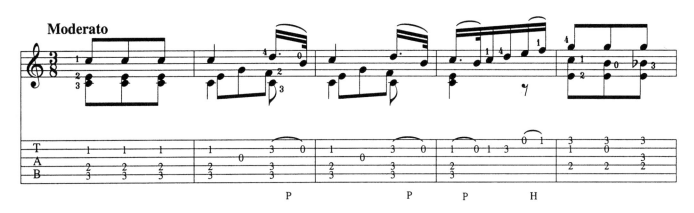

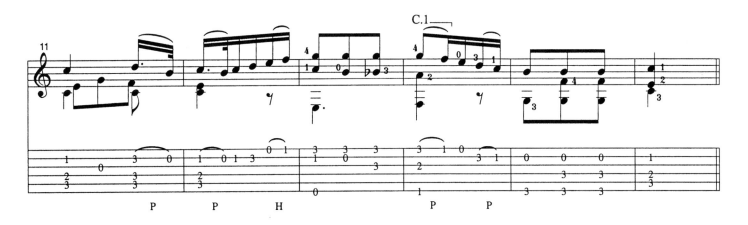

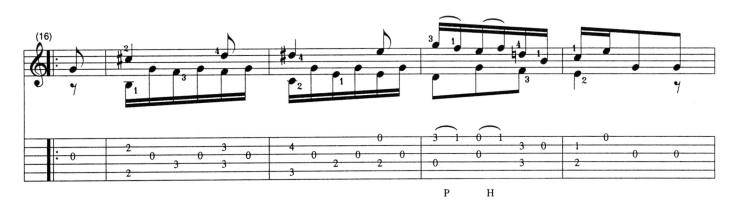

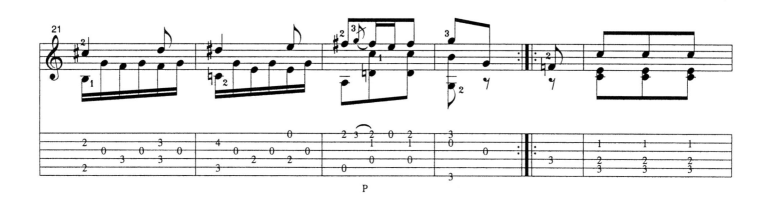

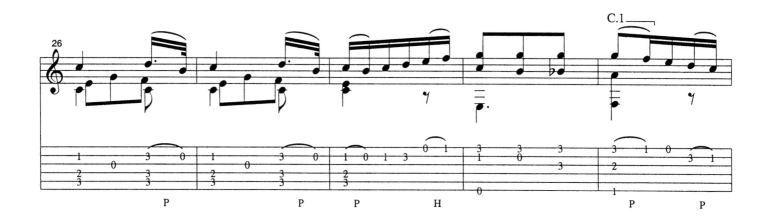

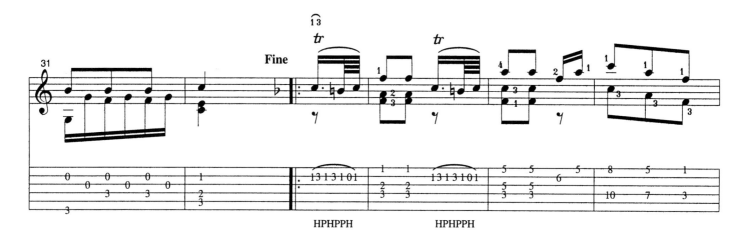

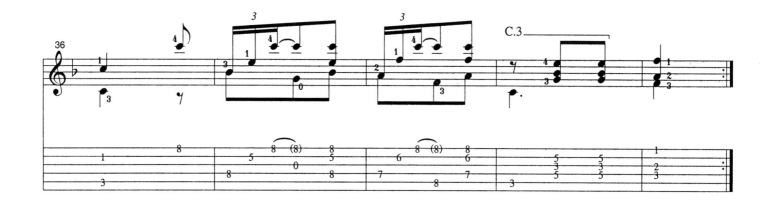

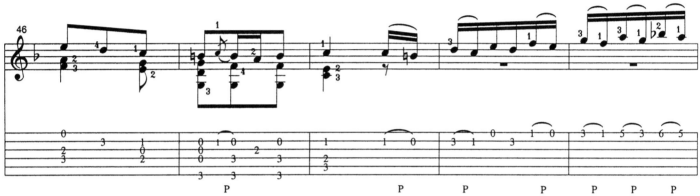

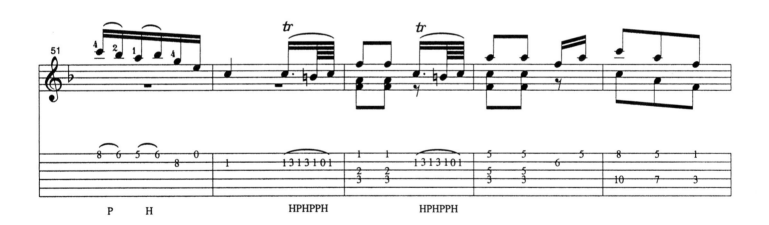

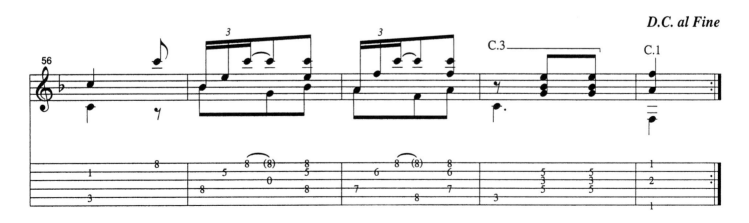

Minuet in D Major
Op. 11, No. 5

Edited and fingered by
Joseph Harris

Fernando Sor
(1778–1839)

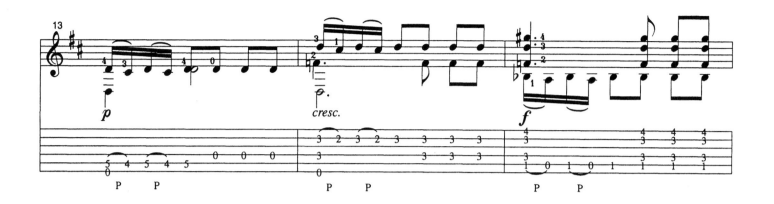

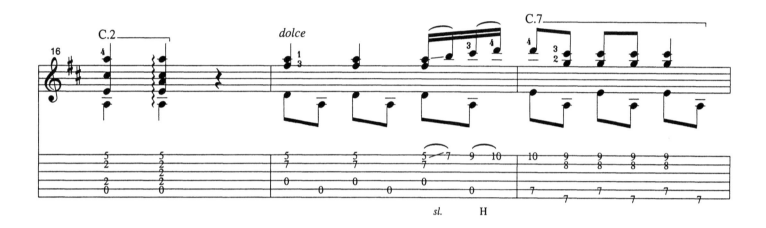

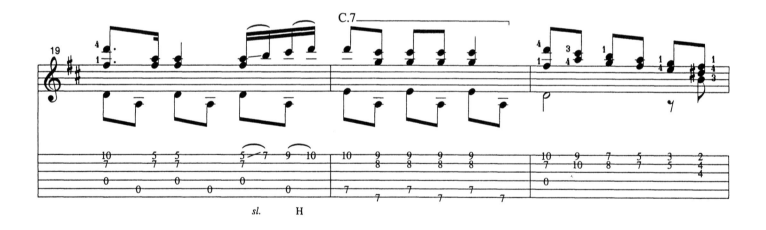

Minuet in E Major
Op. 11, No. 10

Edited and fingered by
Joseph Harris

Fernando Sor
(1778–1839)

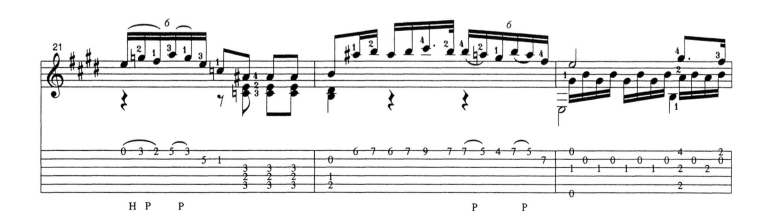

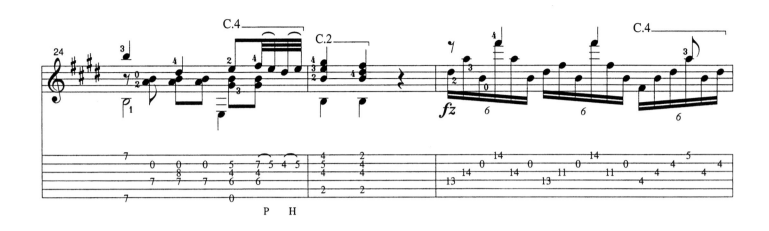

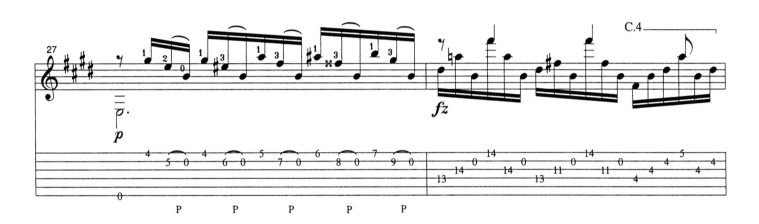

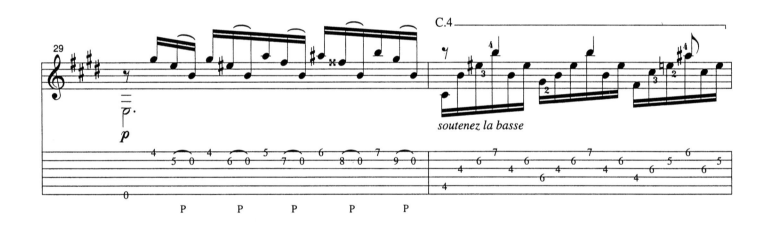

Divertimento in C Major
Op. 13, No. 3

Edited and fingered by
Joseph Harris

Fernando Sor
(1778–1839)

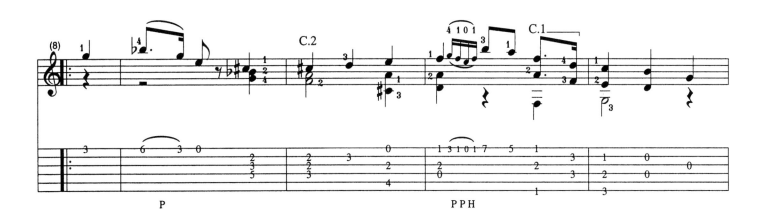

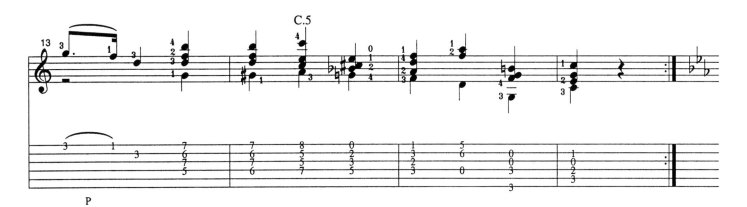

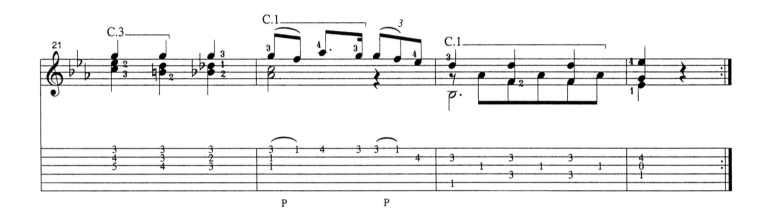

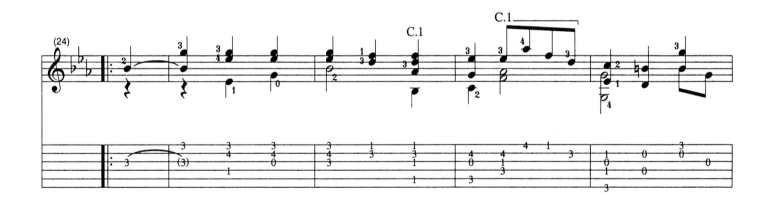

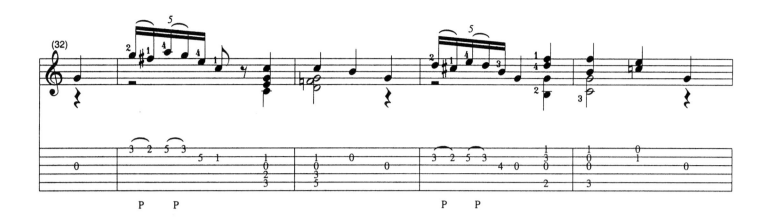
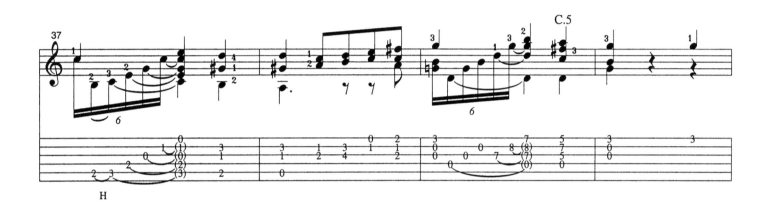

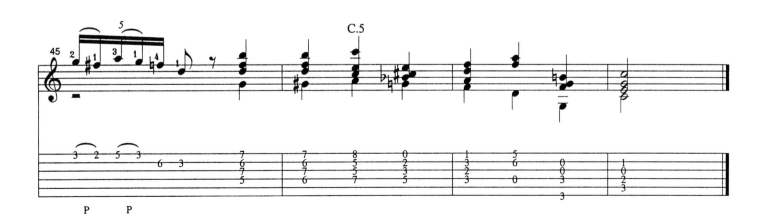

33

Les Folies d'Espagne
Op. 15(a)

Edited and fingered by
Joseph Harris

Fernando Sor
(1778–1839)

Theme

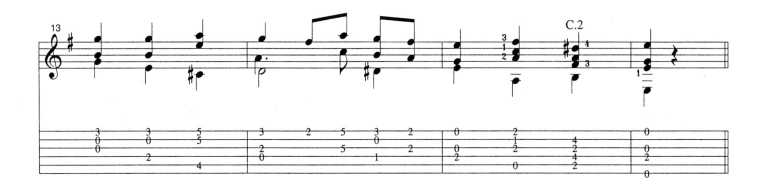

First variation

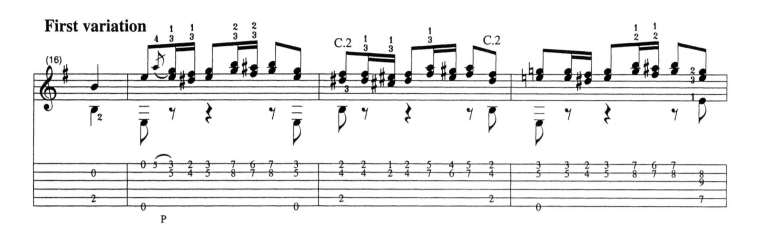

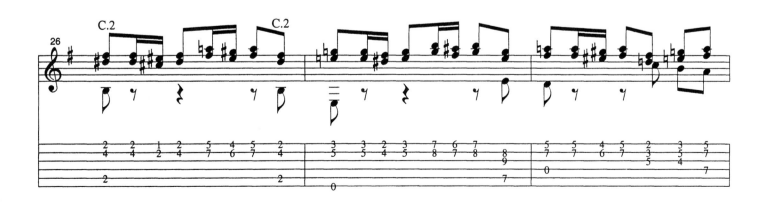

Second variation

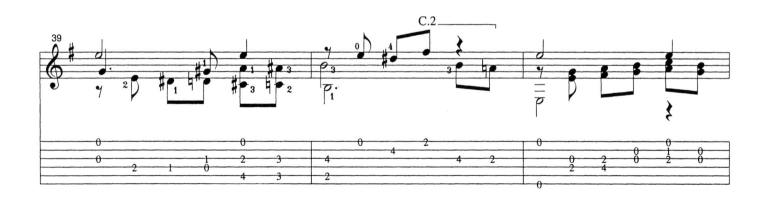

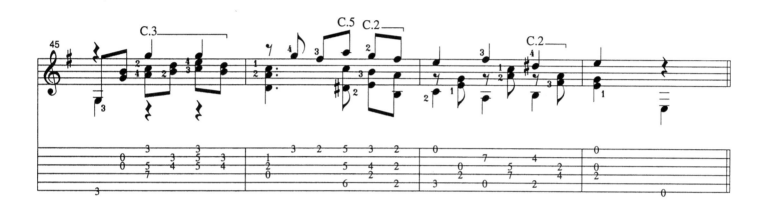

Third variation

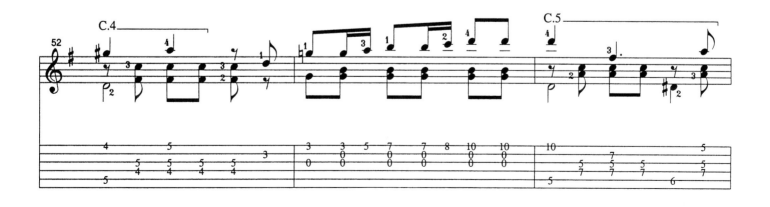

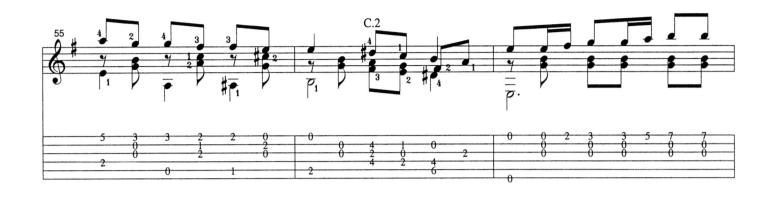

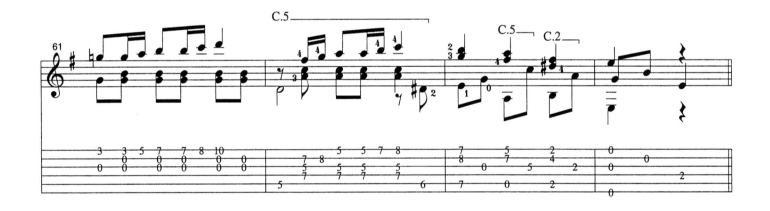

Fourth variation

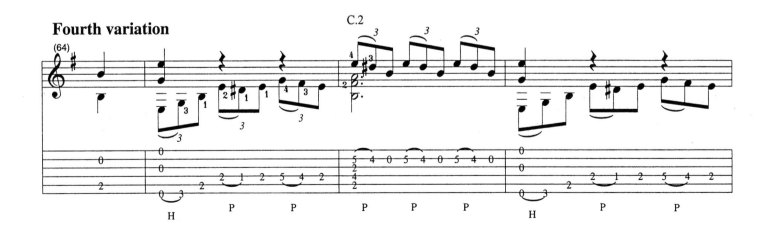

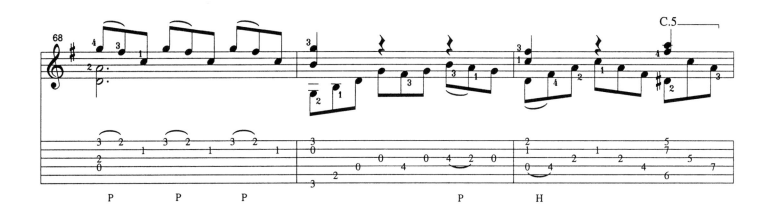

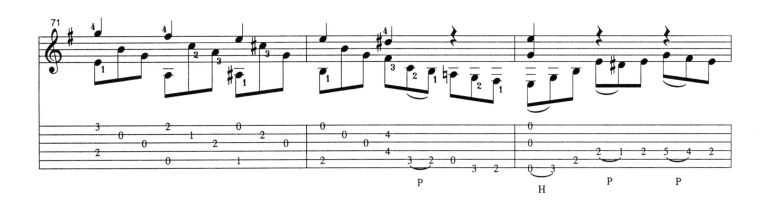

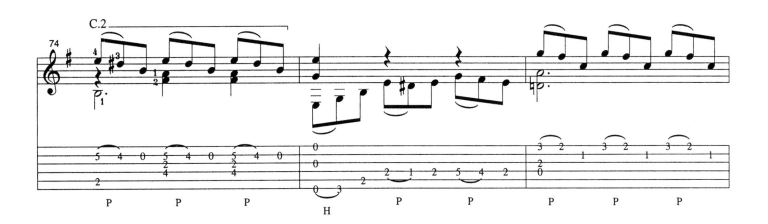

Six Airs from Mozart's *The Magic Flute*
Op. 19

Edited and fingered by
Joseph Harris

Fernando Sor
(1778–1839)

1. Marche Religieuse
Andante

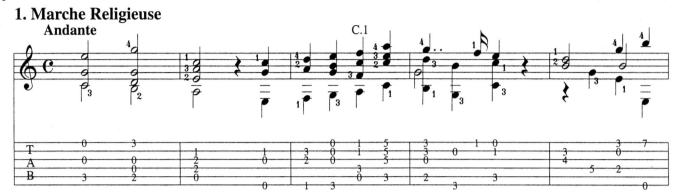

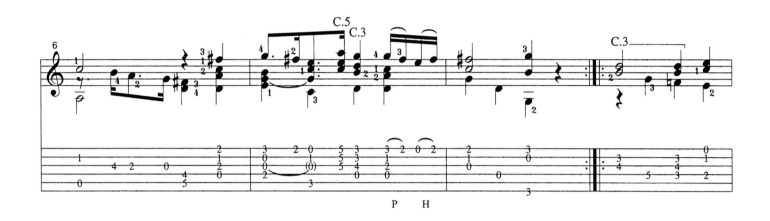

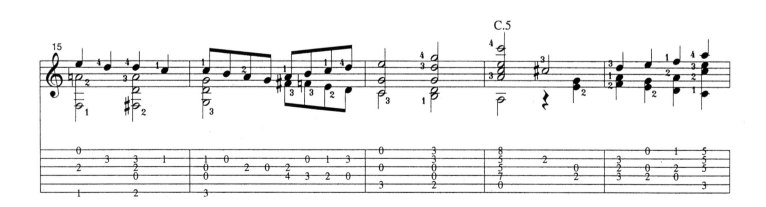

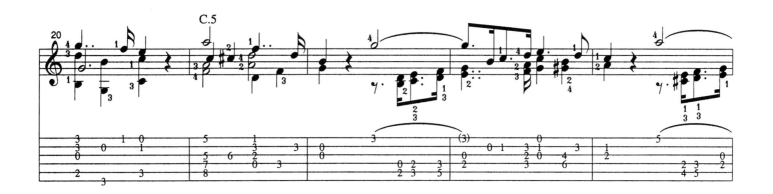

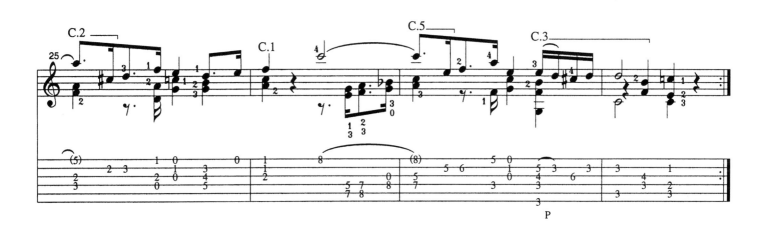

2. Fuggite o voi belta fallace

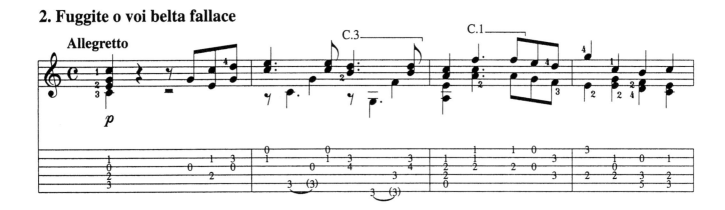

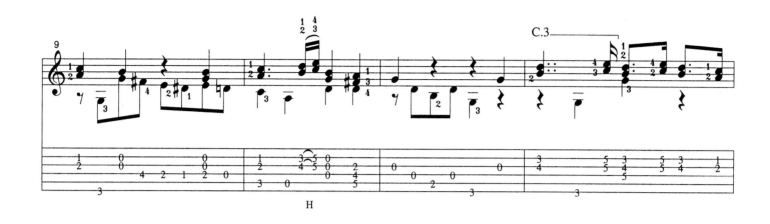

3. Giu fan ritorno i Geni amici

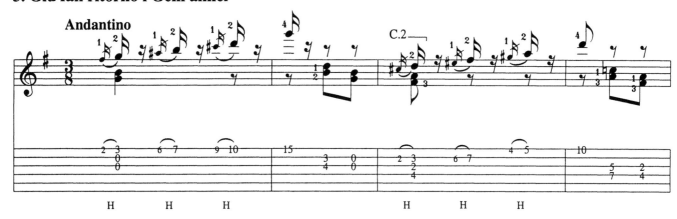

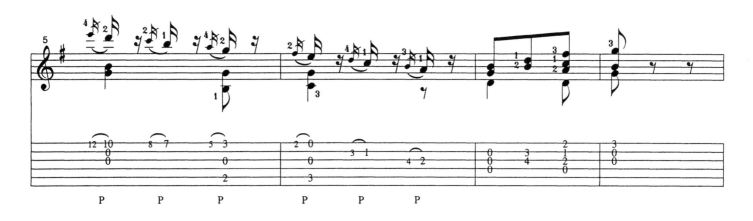

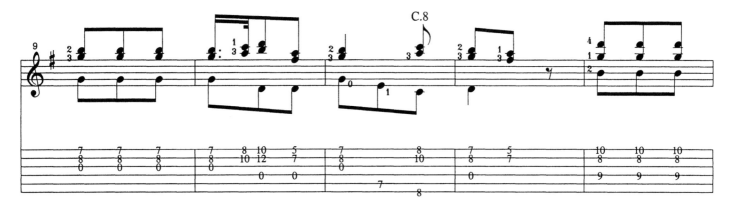

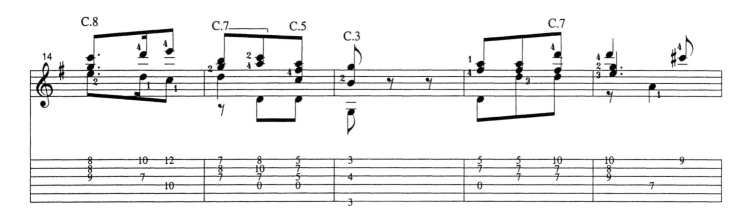

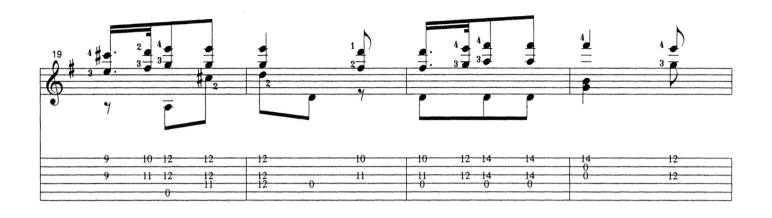

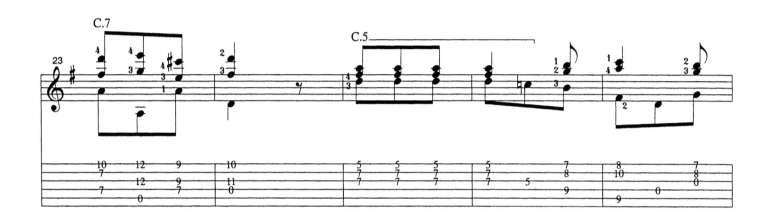

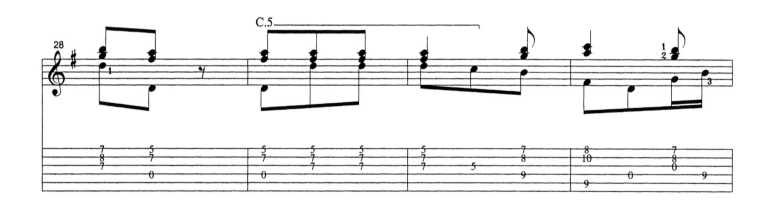

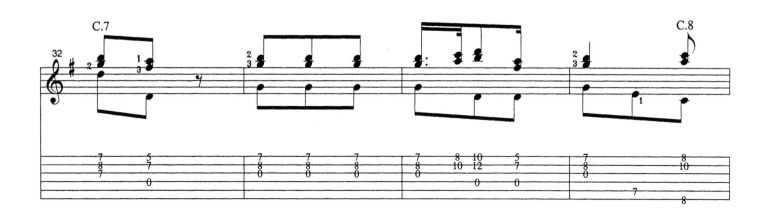

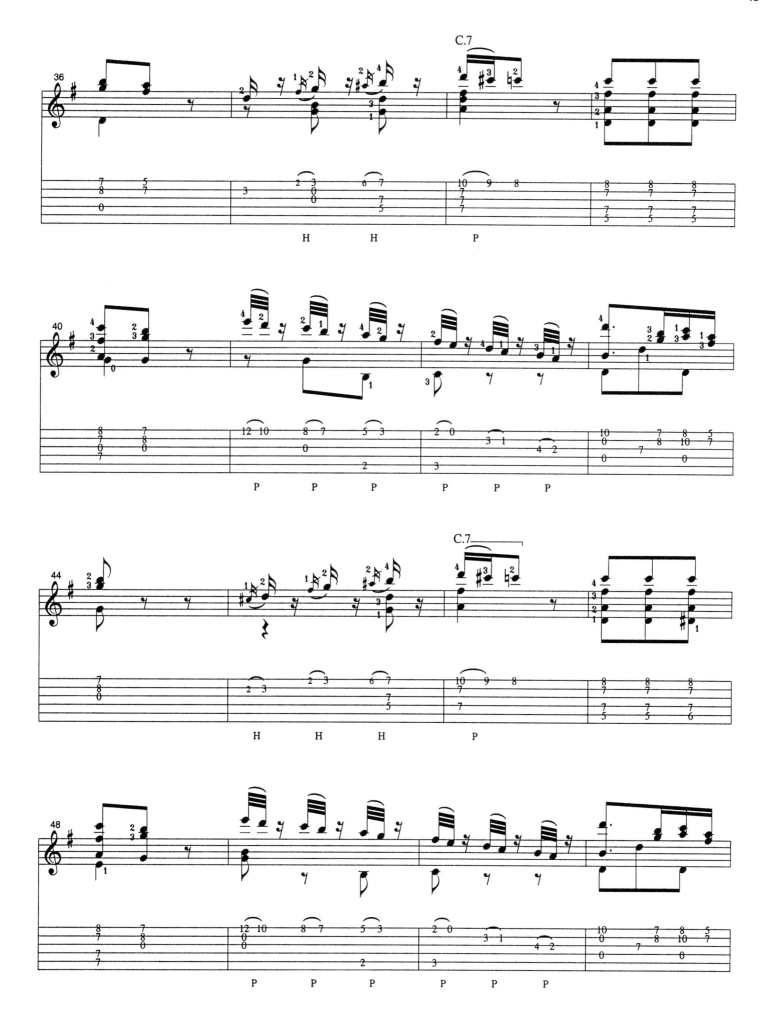

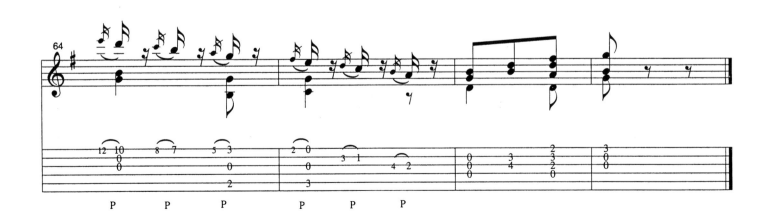

4. O dolce harmonia

Andante

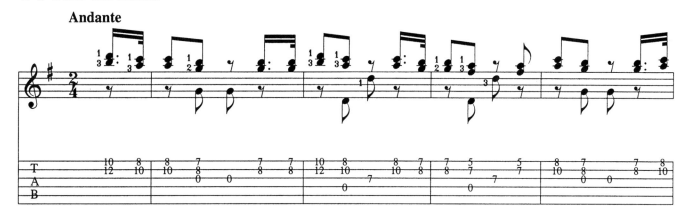

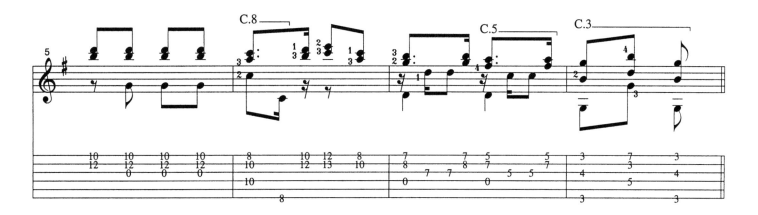

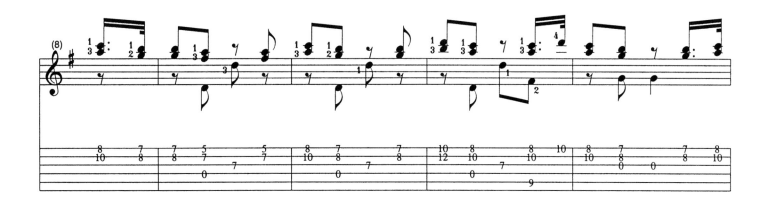

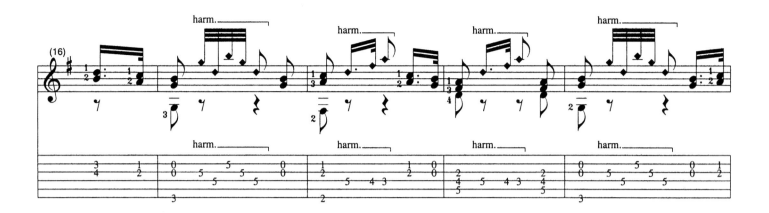

5. Se potesse un suono, etc.

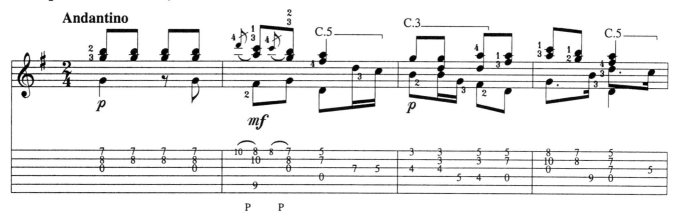

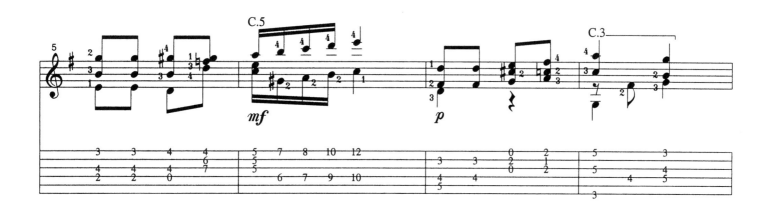

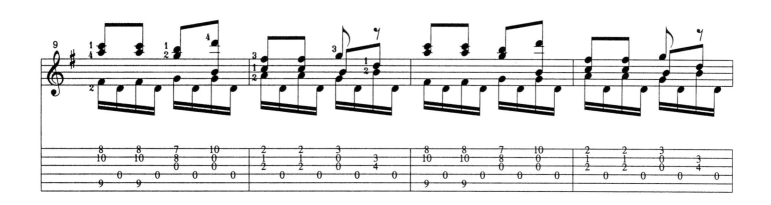

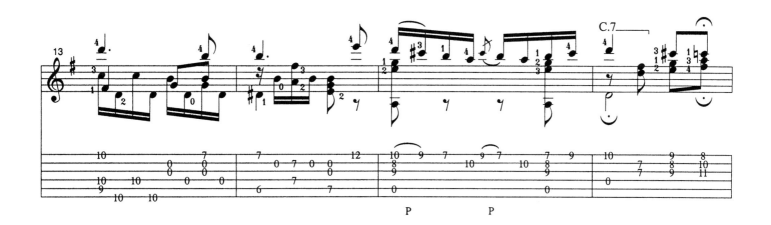

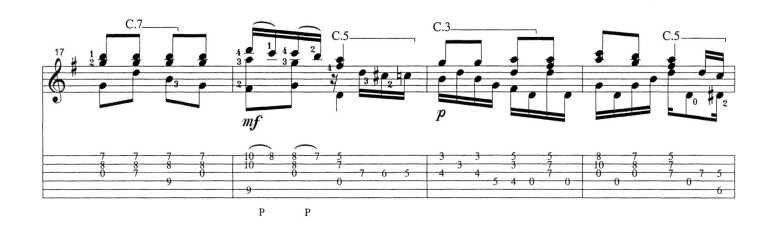

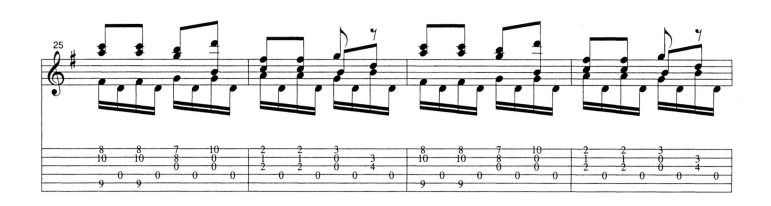

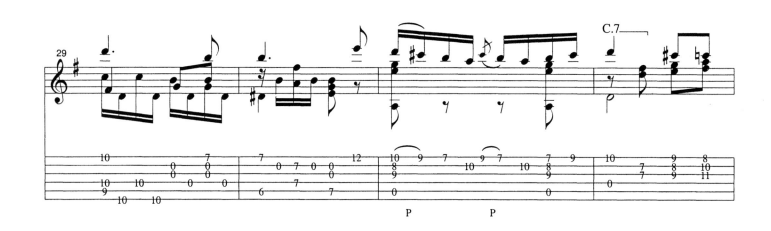

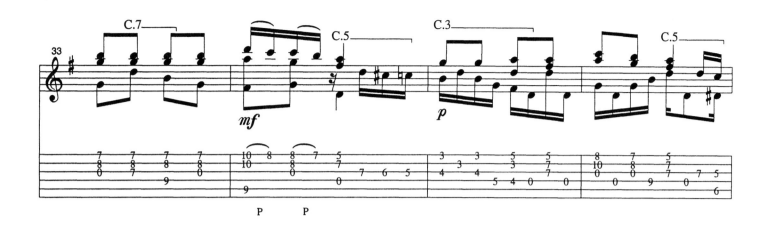

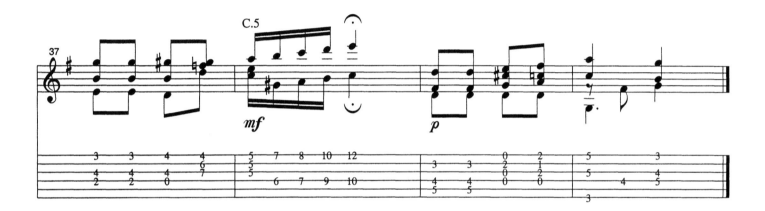

6. Choeur: Grand Isi grand' Osiri

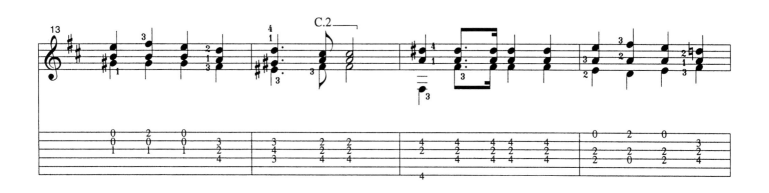

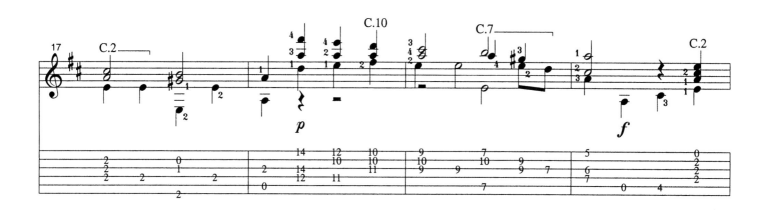

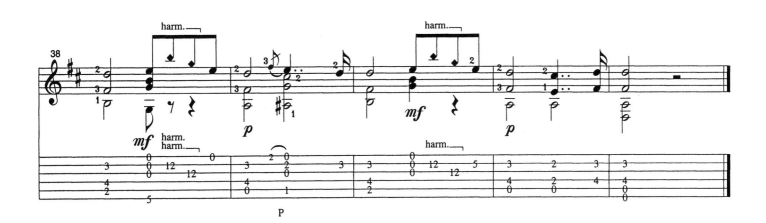

P

Fantasia in E Minor
Op. 21 ("Les Adieux")

Edited and fingered by
Joseph Harris

Fernando Sor
(1778–1839)

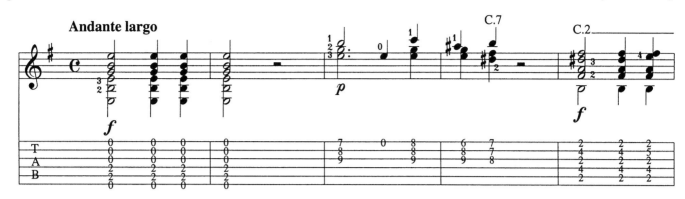

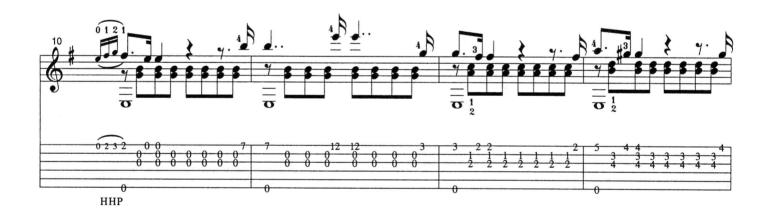

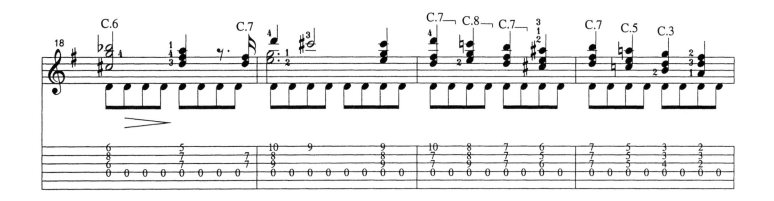

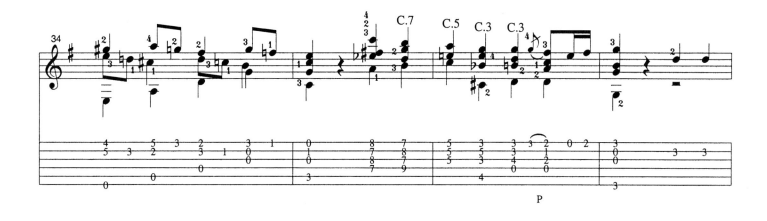

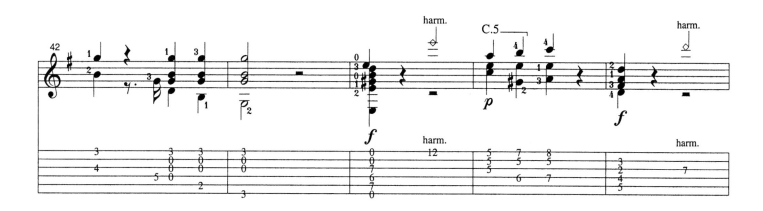

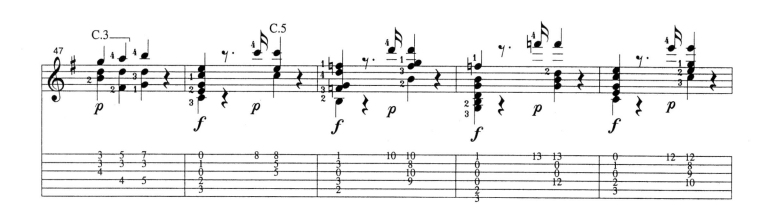

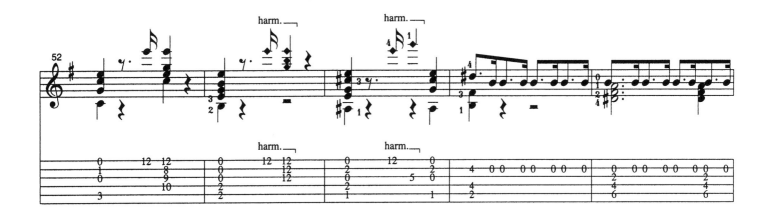

58

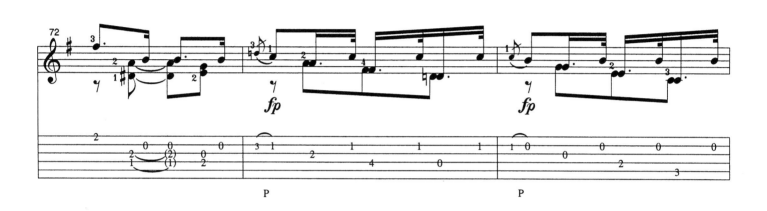

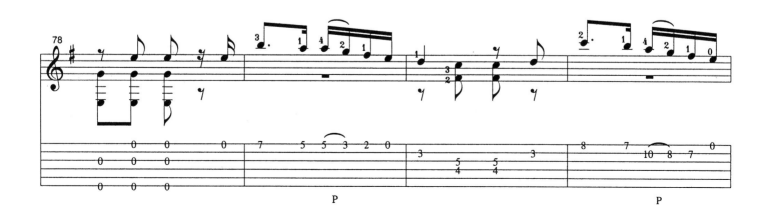

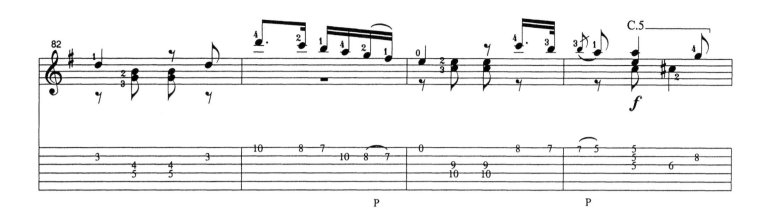

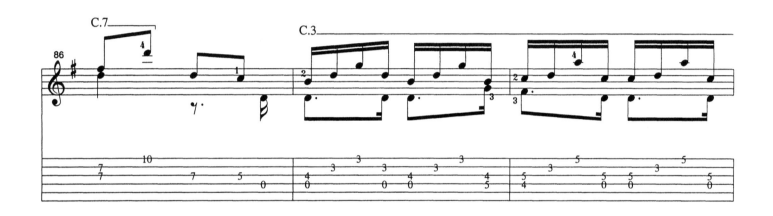

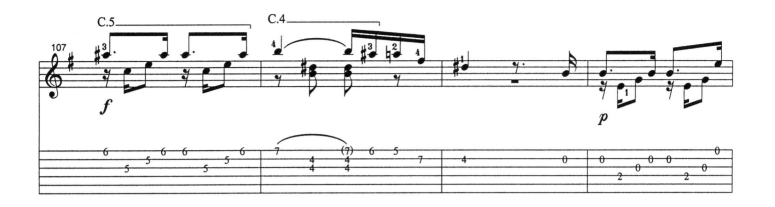

Minuet in C Major
from Grand Sonata, Op. 22

Edited and fingered by
Joseph Harris

Fernando Sor
(1778–1839)

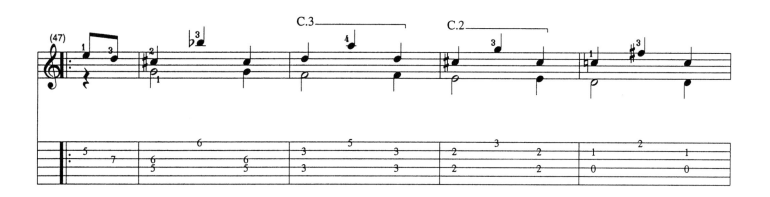

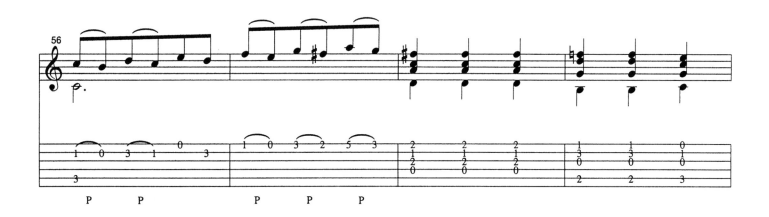

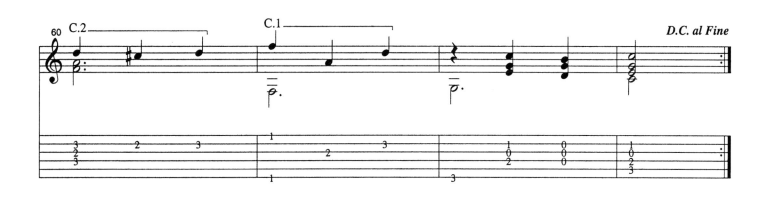

Petite Pièce in A Major
Op. 45, No. 3

Edited and fingered by
Joseph Harris

Fernando Sor
(1778–1839)

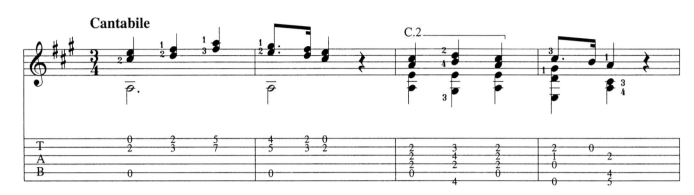

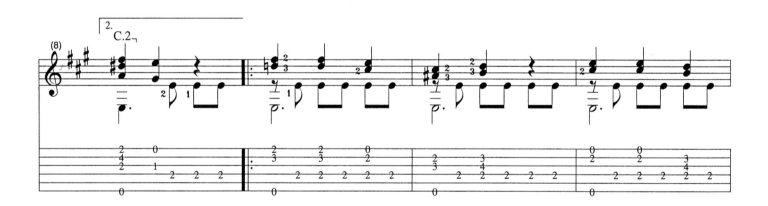

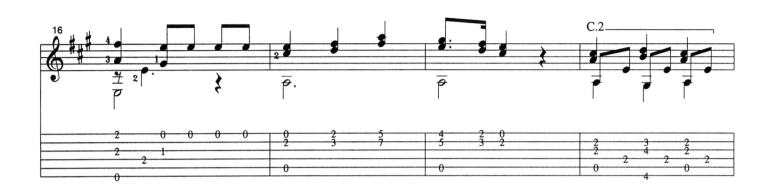

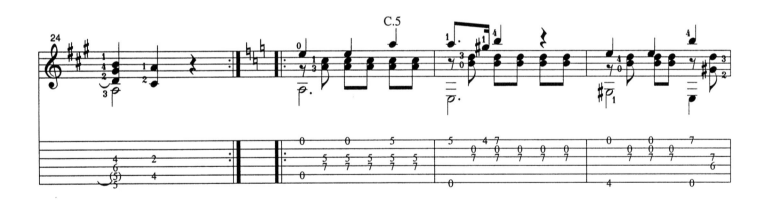

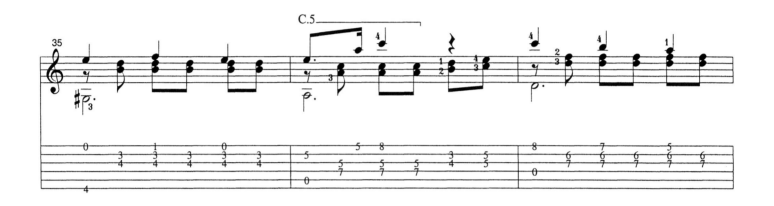

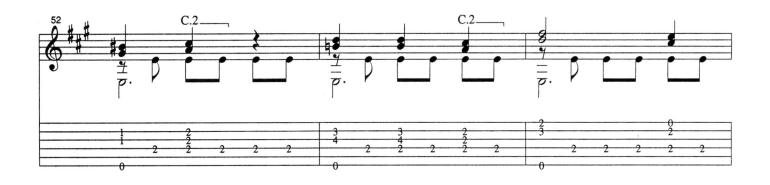

70

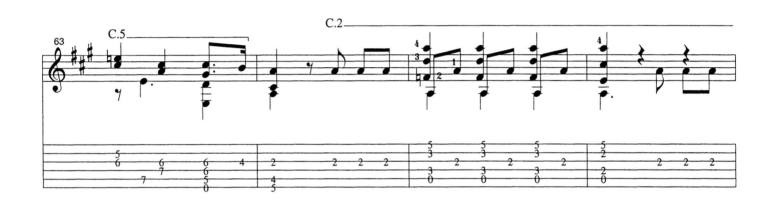

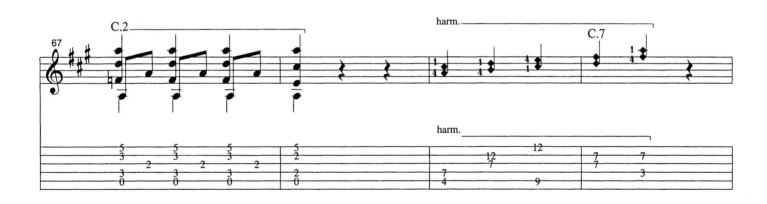

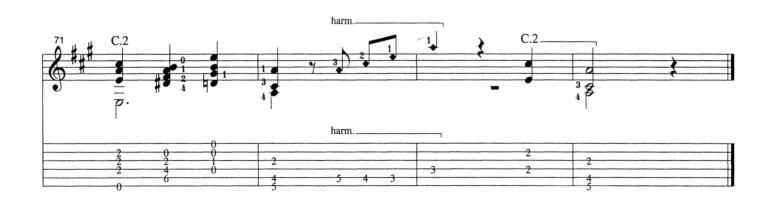

Study in D Major
Op. 29, No. 21

Edited and fingered by
Joseph Harris

Fernando Sor
(1778–1839)

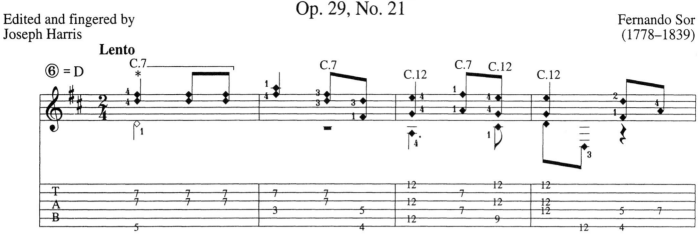

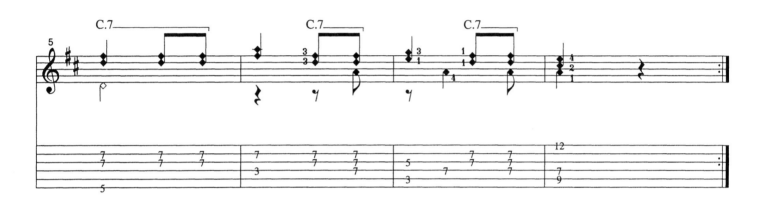

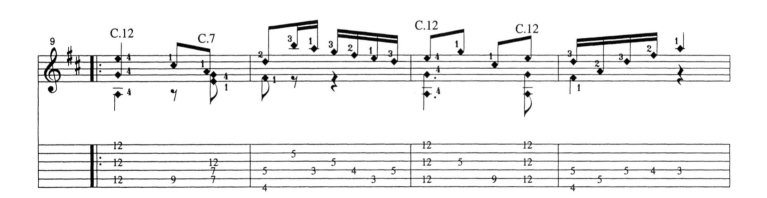

*Play all notes as natural harmonics.

Petite Pièce in A Major
Op. 45, No. 5

Edited and fingered by
Joseph Harris

Fernando Sor
(1778–1839)

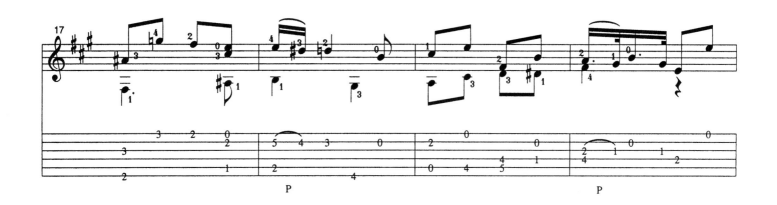

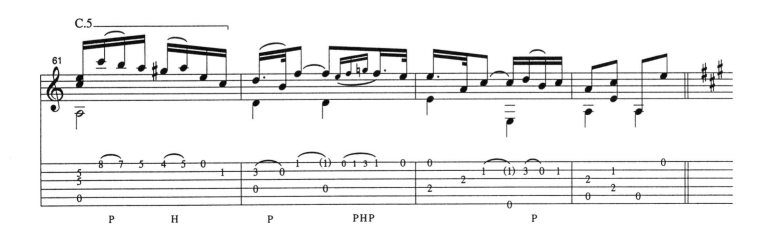

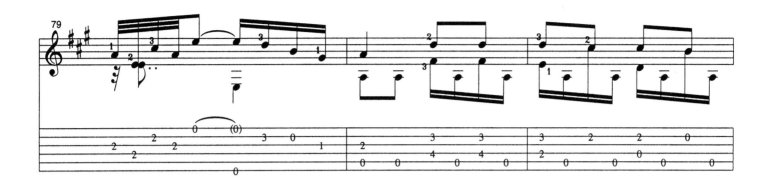

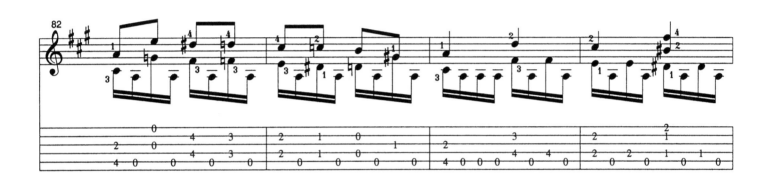

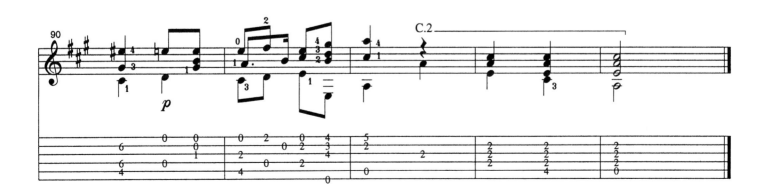

Minuet in G Major
(c. 1810)

Edited and fingered by
Joseph Harris

Fernando Sor
(1778–1839)

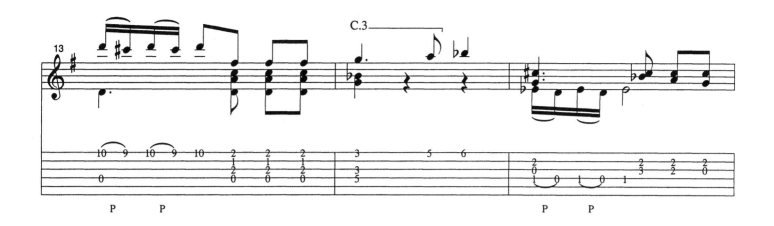

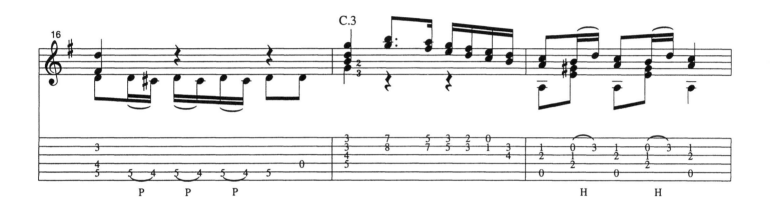

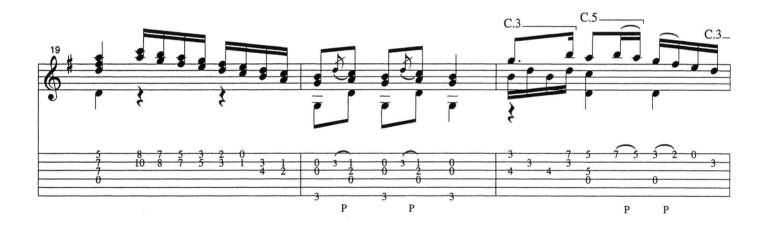

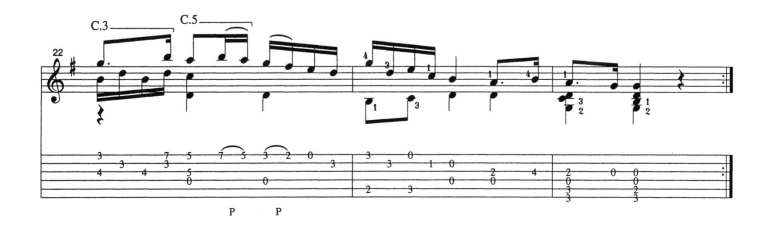

Bagatelle in D Minor
Op. 43, No. 5

Edited and fingered by
Joseph Harris

Fernando Sor
(1778–1839)

P P H

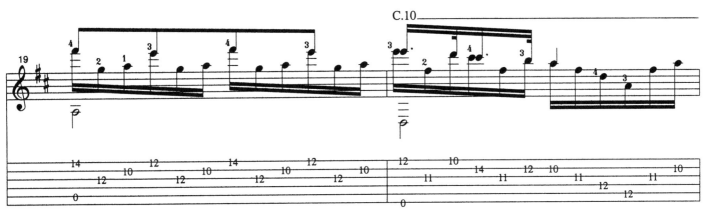

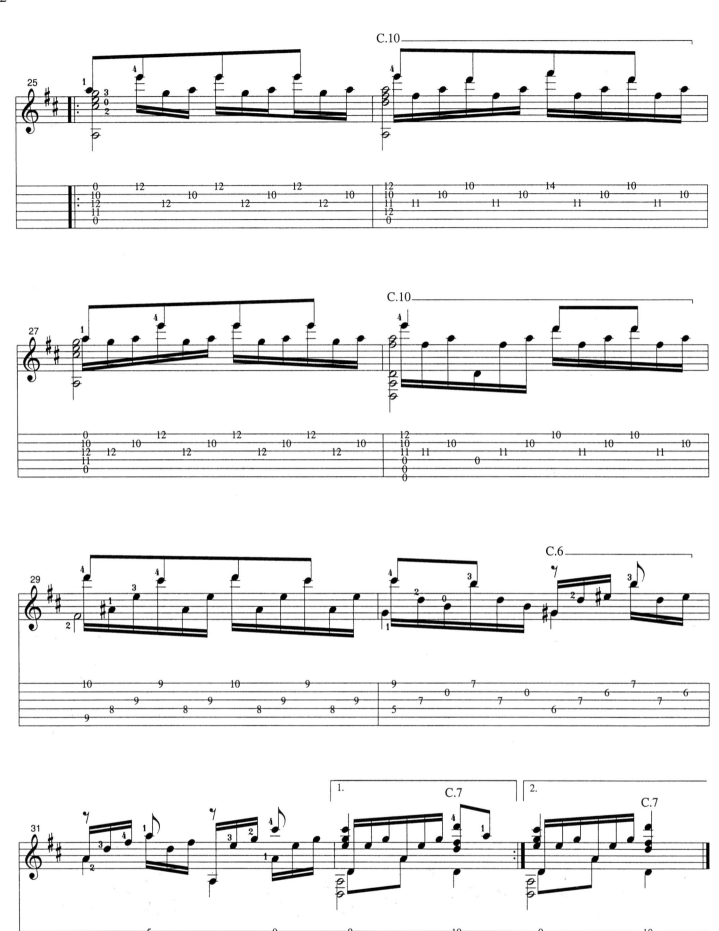

Study in E Minor
Op. 6, No. 11

Fernando Sor
(1778-1839)

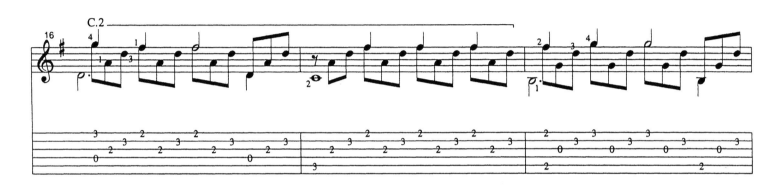

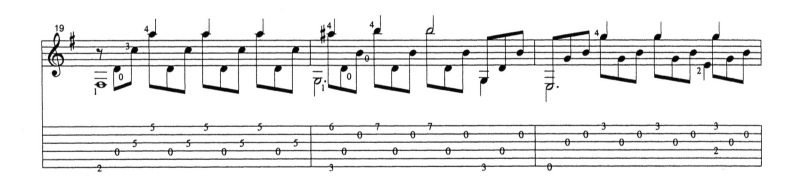

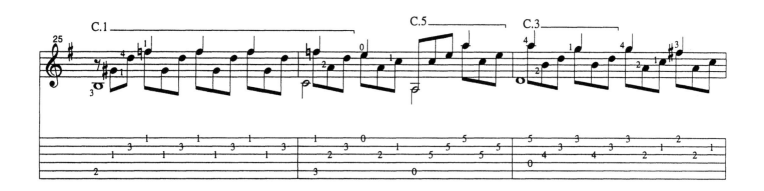

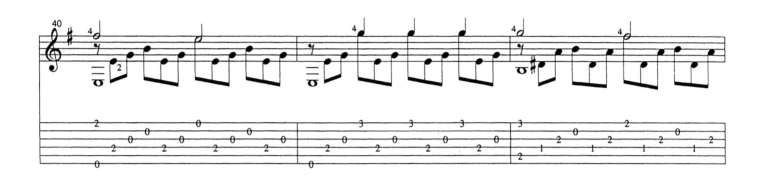

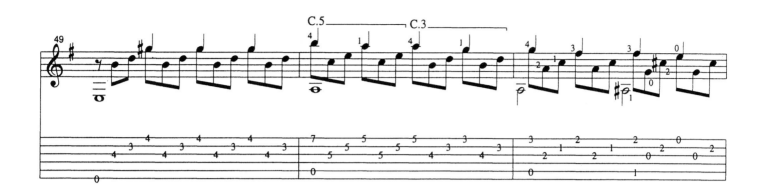

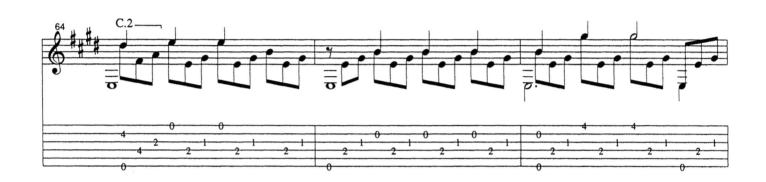

Leçon in D Major
Op. 31, No. 10

Edited and fingered by
Joseph Harris

Fernando Sor
(1778-1839)

Cantabile

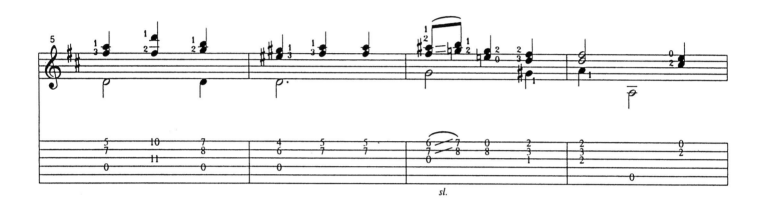

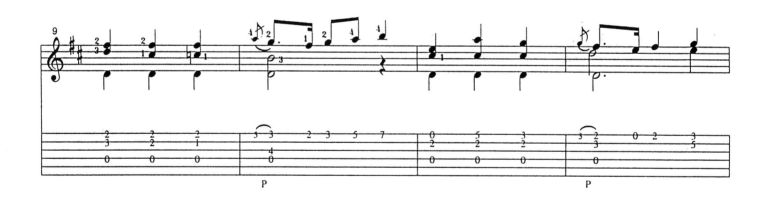

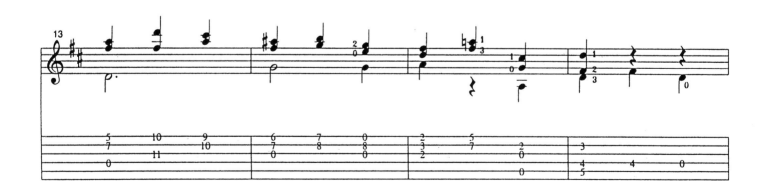

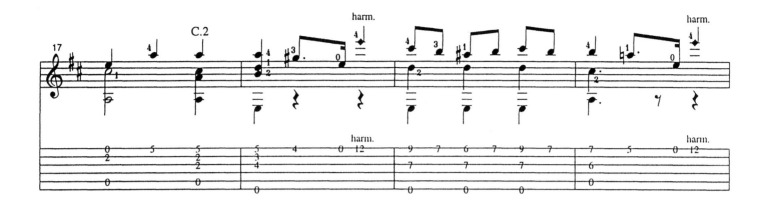

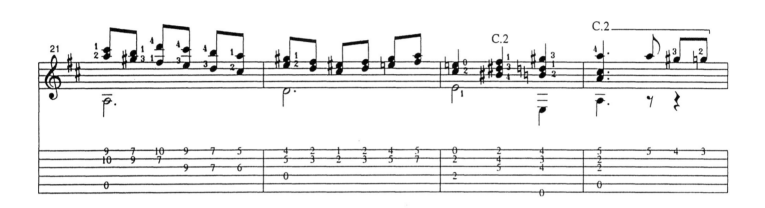

Leçon in E Major
Op. 31, No. 23

Edited and fingered by
Joseph Harris

Fernando Sor
(1778-1839)

Mouvement de prière religieuse

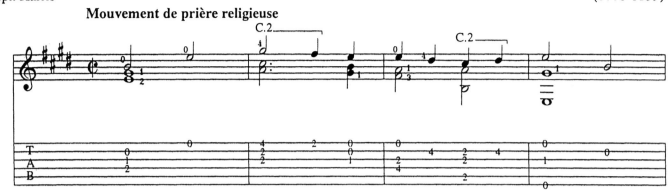

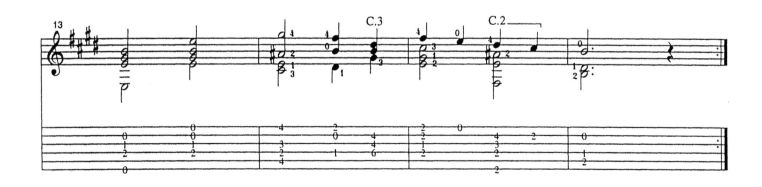

Petite Pièce in E Major
Op. 32, No. 1

Edited and fingered by
Joseph Harris

Fernando Sor
(1778-1839)

Andantino

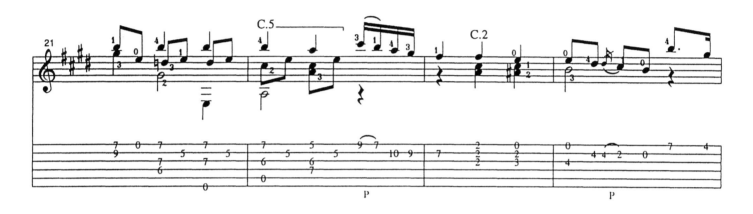

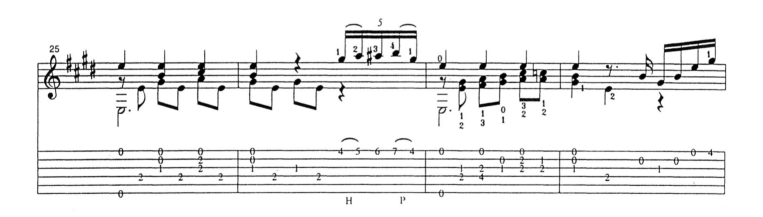

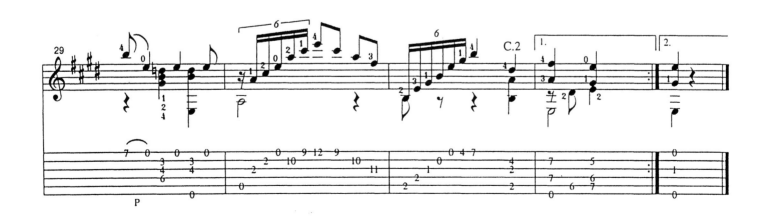

Study in B Minor
Op. 35, No. 22

Edited and fingered by
Joseph Harris

Fernando Sor
(1788–1839)

Minuet in G Major
Op. 2, No. 1

Edited and fingered by
Joseph Harris

Fernando Sor
(1788–1839)

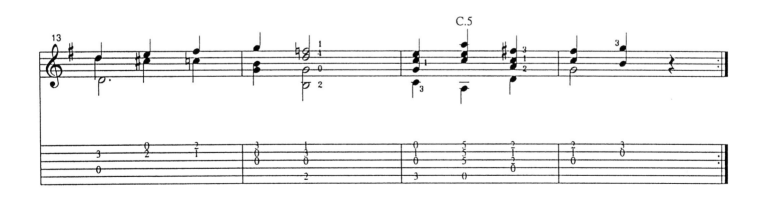

Petite Pièce in A Major
Op. 44, No. 21

Edited and fingered by
Joseph Harris

Fernando Sor
(1778-1839)

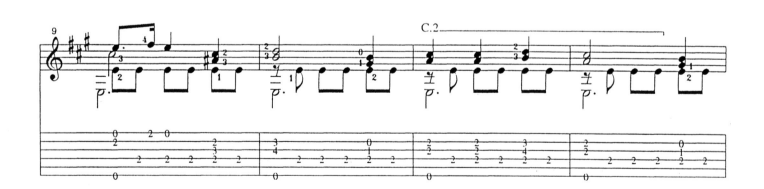

Minuet in A Major
Opus 11, No. 6

Fernando Sor
(1778-1839)

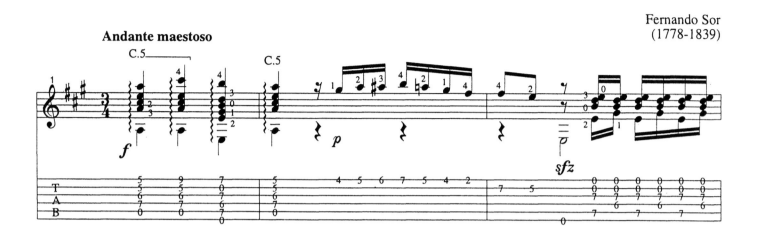

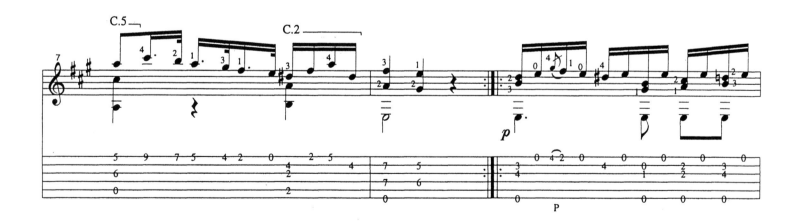

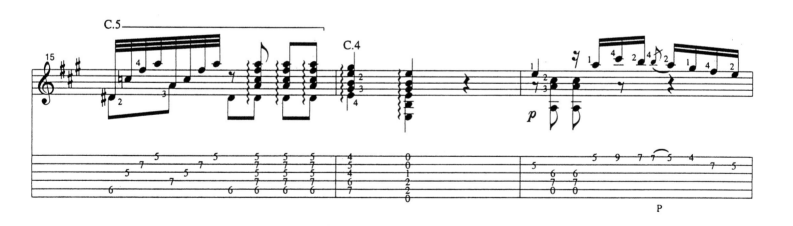